PAUL AND THE LAW OF LOVE

PAUL AND
THE LAW OF LOVE

By

FLORENCE MICHELS, O.L.V.M.

THE BRUCE PUBLISHING COMPANY / MILWAUKEE

NIHIL OBSTAT: JOHN F. MURPHY, S.T.D.
Censor librorum

IMPRIMATUR: ✠ WILLIAM E. COUSINS
Archbishop of Milwaukee
September 18, 1967

Library of Congress Catalog Card Number: 67–30099

FOREWORD

Christianity is experiencing a twofold crisis, both as a faith which presumes to make explicit something of God's self-revelation to men and as an ethos which specifies what man's conduct should be in response to this revelation. Those who preach or teach Christianity in any formal way — whose mode of spreading the gospel is verbal, that is to say — realize that the exposition of the mystery of God's love is nearly impossible unless some insights are supplied into human behavior. Conversely, the mystery of ethical concern proves all but impossible to expound unless it can be grounded on some credible base of the mystery of God's love. In brief, both doctrine and morality are having heavy weather in today's Church, and their fates are inextricable from each other.

Yet even when the realization has been reached of the interaction between God's holiness and man's wholeness, there is not ready to hand a large body of writing on the points of intersection between the two. Roman Catholics in particular suffer from a lack of literature in this field. They are generally convinced that "love of God and neighbor" sums up the whole law, but the Augustinian catechesis on the decalogue has somehow reached them in reverse: they know much about the ten-stringed lyre of the Mosaic commands but relatively little about the Spirit who alone, according to Augustine, can bring music from these strings. The whole history of moral theory in the Roman Church needs to be gone into for an accounting of why this is so. Suffice it to say that the contemporary Catholic is beginning to realize that his moral theory must derive from the Bible if it is to be Christian. Yet when he is faced with a position attributed to Jesus or to his disciple Paul he is likely to throw up his defenses by reminding everyone within earshot (starting with himself) that liberty is not license.

v

Liberty indeed is not license. Liberty is liberty. And liberty in Christ is in painfully short supply among Christians because the teaching of St. Paul — its chief expositor after the Master — is not well known. This volume of Florence Michels, a skilled catechist and trained theologian, does much to make the Pauline teaching better known. The work is subtle but it is not imprecise; it is complex but it is not confused. This is so because the moral theory of Paul is not a simple matter and the author reflects that theory faithfully.

At times one can envision the reader who is in search of instant wisdom saying impatiently, "Why can't she say what she means?" She does, but the difficulty is that she is saying what Paul means and he means a great variety of things. One does not report on a tapestry in a paragraph. Largeness of conception requires largeness of summation. The Pauline synthesis was arrived at by dialectic and not everyone has the time, or takes the time, to follow the dialectical process. It proves a rewarding investment, however, for anyone who does.

The present work is an invitation to examine the best Pauline scholarship of the past few decades to discover the deepest meaning of that opposition between liberty and law one hears so frequently mentioned. Pauline faith and hope and charity are all part of the context in which the problem is set. No thematic problem is disregarded by the writer in her attempt to make a complete report.

Her own conclusions, when they come, are highly nuanced. Surely this will not please every reader. Even when she summons the witness of several modern students of human behavior, no fullscale, clearcut catechesis of morality is forthcoming. She disappoints false hopes every time.

Dr. Michels, or Sister Florence as you will, fulfills the only legitimate hope one should entertain in doing business with a book of this sort. She provides essential New Testament background to the problems of modern morality. Like Paul she situates them in the only place she can, namely the Christian conscience where the individual — who is not a monad but a member of a faith community — learns both his resources in Christ and what is expected of him in the way of behavior. After a personal dialectic which is unavoidable, he acts freely and in good conscience.

To do so is the invitation of this book.

GERARD S. SLOYAN
Professor of Religion
Temple University

INTRODUCTION

Religious educators today are engaged in a searching evaluation of their performance. Their not entirely successful efforts to show the relevance of the Christian message to the contemporary situation have led them to a serious questioning of their methods and of the content of their message.

This healthy dissatisfaction has been particularly evident in the field of morality. Catechists are concerned when they see developing a negative kind of religion, its multiple prescriptions giving Christians a certain sense of security which lulls with the force of the potent tranquilizer. A conviction that the spirit of Christ cannot be embodied within a legalistic framework impels the catechist to break out of this confining structure.

At the same time they realize that the goal of all legislation is to help man to act in a more human manner; civil codes induce man to look beyond the level of self-preservation in his actions. But the kind of man these laws beget is a sort of robot, a rigid conformist. The Old Testament introduced an ingredient of love into legislative enactments; therefore conformity to the law of Moses gave man a more human contour. But with time Israel began to regard the Mosaic code as an ultimate. Christ pressed man beyond these limitations into the largeness of life in the spirit which requires no legislation; in the realm of the spirit love is mentor.

In ancient Israel fundamental religious and ethical obligations were codified in six hundred and thirteen legal prescriptions. No one has yet bothered to count the myriad regulations which govern conduct in the average American community. The habit of conforming anesthetizes, with the result that people are not conscious of the many obligations which oppress them. But the tendency to make Christians subservient to the law is as certain today as it was in the days of Jesus and of Paul. Not that today's Christian should abdicate every civil ordinance! But the tendency to conscript the Christian conscience to a new drillmaster is cause for concern. Because the moral education of the younger generation is always an urgent consideration, Christian morality has frequently been couched in terms of a new legalism in which everyone must be trained. The hazards of such an education are insidious. For example, the mechanical conformity demanded by civil rights laws is likely to produce an illusion of Christian justice. But Christ wants men's actions to flow from the dynamic of love, not from the static of law. Christ's challenge: "Can you people love?" demands some response.

The ethics of Paul always seem in danger of opening the floodgates of anarchy and license in the name of freedom from the law. To avoid this danger, Christians have sometime adopted a type of coalition ethics compounded of Judaic, Aristotelian, and Stoic elements. At first sight this compromise has seemed less disturbing and more respectable than a forthright answer to Christ's challenge to love. But the restrictions of such a system effectively inhibit the free response of love which characterizes the communion of the sons of God. Religious educators today are searching for ways of helping Christians to break away from the stranglehold of static restrictions into a more profound existential dimension, a dynamic relationship with the living God and with his brothers. The name for this existential situation is love; it is the active state of being at one with another person.

It would be facile to hold that in Paul's writings a synthesis can be found which will provide a panacea, a bulwark against static and naturalistic presentations of morality which effectively stifle Christian freedom. How convenient a neat formula would be to remedy the ills which have led to the solutions proposed by those who advocate an ethics of situation! However, the problem of an approach to morality which would combine a fruitful confrontation of the problems of this time with a fidelity to the timeless ethic of revealed truth is not so easily solved.

Our purpose here is not to explain with mathematical exactitude the extent to which Christians are freed from the law, nor is it intended as an exact blueprint giving catechetical dimensions for a structure of Christian living. Any valid study of the law must inevitably leave some areas in the realm of mystery. Neither first-century nor twentieth-century terminology can ever hope to explain adequately the law in all its facets; human terms cannot encompass the reality. But a truly religious study of Paul's teaching on the law should lead to a more perceptive understanding of the deepest demands of the law of love.

A freedom born of a personal trust in God through Christ should characterize Christian moral catechesis. That this freedom implies a total commitment of Christians to one another in love, and that this love embraces today's world, is not always evident in moral instruction. To implement this lucid doctrine which is at the heart of Christianity is the purpose of this probing of St. Paul's teaching on the law. An Appendix provides the Old Testament and hellenistic background for Paul's teaching.

CONTENTS

CHAPTER I

ST. PAUL'S ANTITHETIC PRESENTATION OF THE LAW

Ambiguity of Paul's Style

The focus of Judaism in the first Christian century was practical rather than credal. Great latitude was allowed in adherence to doctrine so long as one followed exactly the prescriptions of the torah. In a certain sense Paul's reaction to this legalistic principle was unique. Rather than attempting to distinguish between primary and secondary duties, Paul questioned whether man's relationship to God could be interpreted in terms of law at all.

The rich ambivalence of Paul's view of the law must have seemed to his contemporaries galling and heretical. Paul's wrestling with the ideal of his pharisaic days, namely, the possibility of attaining to righteousness by works of the law, made comprehension of his dialectic more difficult.

The paradox that true righteousness is not the product of man's effort and yet cannot exist in the absence of effort, befuddled minds accustomed to thinking in strictly legalistic terms. They knew that they had to strive for righteousness, but they could not accept their inability to attain it. They were ready to buy the gift of life, but the fact that it could be given only to those ready to spend all they possessed seemed incomprehensible. To acknowledge that the score-

1

keeping induced by legalism was irrelevant in one's personal life was too much for the average Jewish mind of Paul's day.

Because the Jewish community was unable to weigh each element within the context of the occasions which inspired Paul's precise formulation, it could not appreciate the organic unity of his scattered theology. Had the Jewish community probed deeply enough into these formulations it would have caught, beyond the words, the throb of life, the faith, the hope, and the love of a man who had only one thought, one basis of security, and one joy: Jesus Christ, his lord and savior. Paul's attitude to the law, the most intricate doctrinal issue in his theology,[1] was the most misunderstood facet of his teaching.

The ancients, however, were not the only ones with uncomprehending minds; even today the essential balance in Paul's thought is easily missed. Indeed, the possibility must be considered that many contemporary writers reflect a serious degree of muddled thinking and of unexamined assumption regarding Paul's attitude toward the law.[2]

In his discussion of the law, Paul was more concerned with content and meaning than with the manner in which he expressed his message. Vitality compensated for stylistic elegance, but the consequence was a certain ambiguity, particularly when one attempts to translate his message into terms appropriate for the twentieth century.

When Paul wrote of a subject, it was always from a particular existential viewpoint. His moral teachings were not systematized; they were a succession of brilliant flashes, particularly on the relation of the law to the Christian life.[3]

---

[1] H. J. Schoeps, *Paul: The Theology of the Apostle in the Light of Jewish Religious History*, trans. Harold Knight (London: Lutterworth Press, 1961), p. 168.

[2] C. E. Cranfield, "St. Paul and the Law," *Scottish Journal of Theology*, 17:1 (March, 1964), 43, cites examples in recent writings which seem to reflect a need for a thorough re-examination of the New Testament understanding of the law and of the place of the law in the Christian life.

[3] Augustin George, *La Morale de Paul: Etudes Exégétiques* (Paris: Commission des Etudes Religieuses, 1959), p. 7.

The human reduction of salvation to a system of static quantities hardly provides an adequate explanation of the dynamic of Paul's legal polemic. Although modern writers have the right to contrive a synthesis of Paul's thinking on the law, this must be undertaken with a certain distrust of their own intellectual constructions. Otherwise there is danger that an individual writer may produce his own morality and not a synthesis of Paul's moral teaching.

What Paul wrote expressed what he meant. However, the difficulty in interpreting Paul's writings has led to widely diverse opinions. The problem is partly one of language. The problem of understanding the language of an ancient culture has augmented the difficulty of translating important distinctions in meaning from one culture to another. In the case of Paul, however, the problem of language was even more complicated. His cultural environment was hellenistic and his language was Greek, but his religious heritage was hebraic. Although Paul used the Greek language to express his thoughts, his words and phrases persistently suggested hebraic rather than Greek connotations. For example, one might legitimately question whether Paul's use of the Greek word *sárx* conveys the hellenistic idea of the inherently sinful nature of the flesh[4] or the more hebraic notion of flesh as man's index of frailty, that frailty which comes from being made of dust.[5]

Paul's predilection for writing in antitheses compounds the problem. One of his favorite ways of announcing the mystery of divine revelation was to propose two contradictory themes without being much concerned with showing how they could be harmonized. Rather than present a carefully-worked-out synthesis, Paul preferred to formulate with vigor, even risking apparent self-contradiction, believing that

---

[4] Herbert Gale, *The Use of Analogy in the Letters of Paul* (Philadelphia: The Westminster Press, 1964), p. 10.

[5] Claude Tresmontant, *A Study of Hebrew Thought*, trans. Michael Francis Gibson (New York: Desclée Co., 1960), p. 108.

men of faith would know how to weigh the single statements in the light of the whole gospel.

The dominant antithetic rhythm of Paul's writings seems not to have come from a desire for literary style. Paul's literary style appears rather to be the consequence of his complete and utter involvement in the message of the gospel. The surge of antithetic rhythm on the surface is but a sign of turbulent depths.[6] Although he laid the foundations for a reinterpretation of the relevance of the law to the Christian life, Paul never worked out the full implications of his principles. His pharisaic habit of regarding the law as a means of justification, though consciously rejected after his conversion, nevertheless is manifest in an antithetic cadence which is sometimes ambiguous, always forceful.

One of the basic weaknesses of many current attempts to interpret Paul's teaching on the law lies in a superimposition of modern categories on Pauline teaching. Casting Paul's thought in a modern framework risks invalidating the synthesis. On the other hand, Pauline legal teaching must be given contemporary expression. Paul's teachings were eminently timely in the first century, but they certainly contain timeless answers to questions which must ever be answered anew. Dilemmas involving law or spirit, narrowness or freedom, limitation through tradition or creative renewal through faith, work of man or grace of God — for all these exigencies Paul gave guidance which is relevant to the modern situation.

No text dealt more profoundly with the problem of the law than Chapter Seven of Paul's letter to the Romans. Here Paul praised the law as holy; in fact, he designated the law as spiritual. Delighting in the law of God, Paul declared that he was subject to the law as a rational being. The other side of Paul's evaluation of the law is based on his experience of the law as commanding man to act but

---

[6] J. N. Sevenster, *Paul and Seneca, Supplements to Novum Testamentum,* IV (Leiden: E. J. Brill, 1961), p. 26.

giving him no power to perform the required actions. Anomalous situation this, and completely paradoxical, if one did not possess a guide which would lead him through the complexity of Paul's thought even to its origin. This analysis of Paul's antithetic presentation will be pursued in the belief that a study of rhetoric can reveal the mysterious import of a person's deepest meaning.

The Genius of Antithetic Presentation

An inevitable tension between the mind of the writer and the language at his disposal gives rise to a mutually creative situation. On the one hand, a word or even the lack of a word, may mold a man's thinking; on the other hand, the evolution of thought may twist the meaning of a word. This molding and twisting tend to increase the versatility of words at the expense of precision, thus complicating accurate expression.

Paul's letters were written in a language intelligible to the generality of Greek-speaking people; yet to suppose that his language reflected a completely hellenistic background and experience would be to misunderstand it. A strange and awkward linguistic element affecting word meaning and disturbing grammar and syntax lurks in a maze of literary allusions which no ordinary Greek man or woman could have understood. The tension between Jewish heritage and hellenistic environment renders the uniquely Christian concepts that Paul struggled to convey more difficult of comprehension.

Without doubt, word studies constitute one valuable means of penetrating a writer's thought. However, real communication of religious and theological patterns is accomplished by means of larger word-combinations and not by lexical units or words.[7] The sentence and the still larger literary complex

---

[7] James Barr, *The Semantics of Biblical Language* (London: Oxford University Press, 1961), p. 264.

are usually the linguistic bearers of the theological statement. Unlike the word, the sentence is unique and non-recurrent. Every language has a supply of words which may be used again and again; however, no language has a corresponding stock of sentences. When the study of word sequence in individual thought groups is guided by a serious effort to penetrate the message underlying the stylistic features of a writing, one may hope to arrive at the inner core of meaning. Paul's penchant for antitheses, especially in his efforts to grapple with the problem of the law, is a significant literary characteristic that warrants investigation.

Of course, antithetic writing neither originated with Paul nor was it a uniquely hebraic technique. Antithesis is one of the oldest and most effective rhetorical devices. Whereas the origin of antithesis is unknown, the Greeks seem to have been the first to analyze it, to use it extensively, and to formulate rules of usage. The balancing of one idea with another for comparison or contrast suited the Greek temperament; very early they developed special particles to mark balance and antithesis. Paul's formulation was less restrained than that of the Greeks; often it was torrential. In the latter instances Paul had no time for particles; however, even on these occasions he frequently used balance and antithesis as controlling devices.

Hebrew thinking has often been characterized as dynamic and contrasted with Greek thinking which has been designated as static. However, the static-dynamic antithesis does not clearly express the distinction. Only when dynamic thinking is considered the ideal does Greek thinking seem static; an attempt must be made to give positive expression to the antithesis also from the Greek point of view. Perhaps dynamic-resting would more accurately convey the distinction. Greek thinking is characteristically harmonious, moderate, and peaceful.[8]

---

[8] Thorleif Boman, *Hebrew Thought Compared with Greek*, trans. Jules L. Moreau (London: SCM Press, Ltd., 1960), p. 27.

The real distinction lies in the antithesis between rest and movement. However, the rest of the Greek mind should not be thought of as unproductive. This rest leads the Greek to clear, logical knowing, whereas the dynamic of the Israelite leads him to deep psychological understanding. To grasp reality, both kinds of thinking are necessary. Greeks describe reality as *being;* Hebrews delineate it as *movement.* However, reality is both.

Another factor which may affect interpretation of Paul's antithetic presentation warrants comment. Theological writing has manifested a persistent tendency to oscillate between opposite extremes. Attempts to avoid the extremes or to combine divergent antithetic views have given rise to diverse theological doctrines. The repetition of this pendulation seems to indicate that this bent may be inherent in theological thought.[9] This characteristic compounds the difficulty in distinguishing the separate strands of Paul's thought and adds to the uncertainty of ascertaining when he was writing as a Hebrew and when as a man living in a new dimension. Complexity is increased by the fact that Paul was constantly fighting on two fronts; he protested the freedom of Christ against those who wanted to enforce an ancient bondage and insisted upon the law of Christ to those who abused this freedom.

His propensity for taking liberties with logic as well as with syntax may lead one to regard him as a man of two worlds. Yet to think of Paul as a man at home in neither would be utterly to mistake him. While maintaining a relationship with hellenic and hebraic worlds, Paul declared his freedom from both — a freedom in Christ who was lord of each.

Paul's writings cannot be conveniently pigeonholed nor can his thought be closely defined; nevertheless, a skillful use of antitheses effected a certain modulation in the essen-

---

9 Charles M. Mead, *Irenic Theology: A Study of Some Antitheses in Religious Thought* (New York: G. P. Putnam's Sons, 1905), p. 1.

tial continuity of his teaching on the law. It is this modulation as well as this continuum that will be studied; at the
same time we shall note the discontinuity conveyed by Paul's
antithetic vehicle.

Antithesis of Flesh and Spirit

From a superficial point of view, flesh and spirit are
antonyms. For the Greek, these terms contrasted the tangible and the intangible, the contaminated and the pure, the
base and the lofty, the bound and the free. For the Hebrew
the contrast was rather one concerning different aspects of
a single person.

Paul sharply discriminated between the things of God and
the things of man. In distinguishing between flesh and spirit
he leaned heavily upon the Old Testament tradition of the
"Spirit of the Lord" (*ruach-adonai*) as the breath of God
which descended upon man, changed his heart and spirit,
and gave him a new life. However, although Paul used the
language and thought-forms of Judaism, and borrowed from
the Greek world on occasion, he often departed from both;
he modified old ideas and introduced new ones. For example, in his writings the term "spirit" can have one of three
connotations: the Holy Spirit; the merely natural, spiritual
part of man; or this same spiritual part as supernaturalized
by the spirit's presence and action. Therefore, the meaning
of these terms must be determined according to the context
in which they are used. This is at once a difficulty inherent
in Paul's style and an indication of its manifold richness.

As far as his body is concerned, the Christian is still on
earth, still in the flesh.[10] So Paul frequently wrote as though

---

[10] The meaning of the term "flesh" in Paul's writings has been the
subject of much discussion. In *The Semantics of Biblical Language* (London:
Oxford University Press, 1961), pp. 35–37, James Barr takes issue with
John A. T. Robinson's interpretation as enunciated in *The Body: A Study in
Pauline Theology* (London: SCM Press, 1952), pp. 12 ff. Barr contends
that the existence of two terms in a language does not automatically imply
the existence of a philosophical distinction. This is an assumption that Rob-

the Christian were living on two planes or simultaneously in two worlds. The present age and the future age, this world and the world to come, somehow overlap in the Christian experience. The Christian condition is still one of conflict until the whole man has been altogether redeemed and raised. A great cosmic event will terminate the present strife. The mystical element in Paul's thought intensified his non-hebraic opposition between flesh and spirit. However, the opposition between flesh and spirit should not be identified with any antilogy between spirit and body. It is not as if distinct laws governed the two. Although Paul seems to indicate a law in his members which is antagonistic to the law of the spirit (Rom 7:23), this dialectic results from the delicate combination of hellenistic richness of vocabulary and its exactitude in thought and expression which so well complements the more concrete style of the semitic genius.

Romans 7:14–25: The Conflict Between Flesh and Spirit

In this portion of the epistle Paul describes the reality of law and sin, of life and death, by placing spirit and flesh in antipodal relationship. In this passage spirit refers to the Holy Spirit, the power with which God intervenes in the world and in history. The reference to flesh in this instance is simply man, dominated by sin, whose life and works are therefore futile.

---

inson seems to make. However, Robinson does not seem to think that this distinction is crucial for understanding Pauline usage.

It is interesting to note that in a footnote to the very passage to which Barr takes exception, Robinson cites what he regards as Rudolf Bultmann's reading into Paul's thought ideas which are foreign to him. Robinson believes that in *Theology of the New Testament*, Vol. I, trans. Kendrick Grobel (New York: Charles Scribner's Sons, 1951), Bultmann's interpretation of Paul's use of the term "body" is misleading because Bultmann presupposes that Greek distinctions are necessary in the interpretation of Paul's thought.

In spite of these disagreements, it seems to this writer that Bultmann in *Theology of the New Testament*, Vol. 1, pp. 232–239 offers some perceptive observations regarding Paul's use of the term "flesh."

Perhaps most illuminating of all in this connection is a monograph by William Barclay, *Flesh and Spirit: An Examination of Galatians 5:19–23* (Nashville: Abingdon Press, 1962).

In an undulating sweep Paul exonerates the law as the corrupting element, and also clears the material substance of man. Although Romans 7:18 implies that there is nothing good in the flesh, the following verses insist that the real enemy is sin which has found lodging and an avenue of expression in the flesh.[11] Speaking for everyman, Paul wrestles with the enigma caused by obediential discord. But in the midst of his disobedience man must acknowledge that the law is good. A strange power dominates man, a power which binds him to sin.

This passages does not portray specifically either Paul's or mankind's preconversion state or postconversion experience. Rather, it is Paul uttering mankind's great cry of insufficiency. It is Paul's and everyman's realization that only God can untie the fetters of sin and transform a slave into a free man. This is not the recognition of a legalist; rather, it is the abiding realization of the sensitive man of God.

Summing up the situation in 7:21–23, Paul uses the word "law" in two senses. In verse 22 the law is God's law, whereas in verses 21 and 23 the term means principle. Two principles, then, struggle for mastery, and a deadly strife ensues. In a mysterious way the conflict between flesh and spirit explains the strife of the double principle which simultaneously frees and binds. This conflict between flesh and spirit confirms the impotence of the law. But only a study of both sides of the facts will yield a true picture of Christian freedom from the law.

Romans 8:1–14: The Upper Side of the Antithesis

In Romans 7:14–25 emphasis was on the hopelessness of shackled man; now the spotlight is focused upon the capability of the man whom the spirit possesses. The spirit is not a vague, aimless fanaticism, but a spirit operative in order and law. Law and freedom are not antonyms; the law of

---

[11] Richard Longenecker, *Paul: Apostle of Liberty* (New York: Harper and Row, 1964), p. 51.

the spirit creates freedom. Christ brought into the sphere of the flesh the unimpaired power of the spirit which enabled man to fulfill the law (8:4). In this fulfillment superficial legality is gone, but the true law of God's word is satisfied. Those to whom the spirit is given overcome the flesh. The solution of the tension expressed in Rom 7 lies in the direction of the spirit rather than of the law.

In the series of antitheses which follow, 8:6–8 deals mainly with the flesh, and 8:9–11 principally with the spirit. Conduct according to the law of the spirit is possible only for the man who is in the spirit, and conduct according to the flesh stems naturally from existence according to the flesh. Those who live according to the flesh will consistently oppose God and his law because the aim of the flesh is always rebellion.

Flesh (sárx) in this chapter signifies an ethical experience; the implication is unmistakable that a general positive correlation exists between the flesh and evil. Paul is not contrasting life *in* the spirit with life *in* the flesh; rather, he is contrasting life *of* the spirit with life *of* the flesh, or *according* to the flesh. Christ lived *in* the flesh, but he did not live by the flesh. Only God can consummate the change in man from life of the flesh to life of the spirit.

Paul suggests the character of this change by using opposing formulas: living, not "in the flesh," but "in the spirit." Strikingly vivid, these phrases nonetheless resist close analysis. It would seem that these expressions are instrumental and not locative; they indicate a way of life and not a place.

The contrast is quite clear-cut; there is no convenient blurring of margins. The spirit offers the possibility of a new existence if man will open himself and allow the spirit to possess him. Life according to the flesh or life according to the spirit: man must choose one alternative. If he opts for the former, he will be slave to the law; if he chooses the latter, the law of the spirit will free him.

Galatians 5:16–25: Opposition Between the Works of the Flesh and the Fruits of the Spirit

Here Paul effectively highlights the contrast between life of the flesh and life of the spirit. Actually, this portion focuses attention upon the energy of the spirit which breathes new life into man to turn him in a new direction. The spirit turns man aside from the old way of life which was dominated by the flesh.

An interesting concomitant of the new situation appears in the apodictic statement that those in it are no longer under bondage to the law (5:18); they live instead a life rich in faith and love. The Christian is freed from the law, but the law as such is not condemned. Rather, love renders the law irrelevant because in a faith-inspired love that which the law ordains becomes the spontaneous fruit of the spirit (5:18–23). The Christian really upholds the law in the sense that what the law requires appears as the fruit of the spirit. But as law it is extraneous, being superseded by love.

The positive turn of this passage contrasts nicely with the negative emphasis in Romans 7:14–25, and if studied in juxtaposition, these sections can lead one to penetrate ever more deeply the legal reality with which Paul grappled.

Background of Flesh-Spirit Concept in Paul's Writings

In recent years the conviction has grown that the first century milieu within which Paul's writings must be interpreted was variegated and, above all, complex. In particular, it has become increasingly clear that the traditional dichotomy between Judaism and Hellenism was largely false; in the fusions of the first century the boundaries between them seem to have been very fluid.

Jewish and hellenistic thought matured together in the eastern end of the Mediterranean. Both owed a little to Egypt and much to the civilization of the Tigris-Euphrates valley. The Aegean culture also contributed some of its characteristic flavor to both.

The discovery of the Dead Sea scrolls has emphasized further the intricacy of Paul's environment. Far from being homogeneous, the Judaism of Paul's time included some who shared the dualism normally associated with Greece and Persia. Indeed it is possible that the Qumran sectaries derived their dualistic tendencies from these sources.

In general, it seems certain that the Jews did not live in a state of cultural isolation; Jewish and gentile cross-fertilization resulted in an extremely complex milieu. Paul's Judaism was not the orthodox variety current in Palestine. Rather, it was the Judaism of the diaspora, tinged with Hellenism through the use of the Greek language and the consequent adoption of certain Greek modes of thought. However, Paul's was still a pharisaic Judaism, firmly rooted in the law and the prophets.[12]

Although Paul's synthesis was uniquely Christian, extraneous influences can be discerned in certain areas. For example, Paul's understanding of the relationship between flesh and spirit had certain affinities with that of the sectaries.

In some passages of the scrolls (DSD 11:12, for example) the flesh is so closely associated with evil that the term seems to denote the morally lower nature of man. In 11:9 the "company of erring flesh" is parallel to "wicked humanity." The sectaries seemed to believe that belonging to the flesh meant belonging to the sphere of the spirit of darkness. However, a hellenistic dualism is not evident in the scrolls. In the scrolls, existence in the flesh does not in itself signify perversion as it did to the Greeks. Likewise, in hellenistic thought the purification of the flesh was not sought; because the flesh was regarded as evil, escape from it was desired.

---

12 Frederick C. Grant, *Roman Hellenism and the New Testament* (New York: Charles Scribner's Sons, 1962), p. 146.

Where Paul uses this term with a moral connotation,[13] "flesh" seems to be very close in meaning to the sectarian usage. Assuredly, in his polemic against sectarian ideology, Paul used the language of his opponents (as evidenced by Col 2:11, 13, for example). But although the scrolls supply an added clue to the connotation of the terms that Paul used, their sectarian meaning was not determinative of the Pauline mode.

The ethical dualism of the sectaries was expressed in terms of two spirits, whereas in Paul it was communicated in terms of the antithesis of flesh and spirit. Nowhere in the scrolls was the flesh equated with the spirit of error; rather, the flesh was delineated as the sphere within which the spirit of error worked. Therefore, the parallelism between Paul and the scrolls on this point is loose. Assuredly, Paul shared the sectarian terminology at certain points, but he did not share its doctrinal formulations.

Paul believed in the continuity of the spirit in the old and new dispensations. However, his emphasis was not on this aspect. In setting the law in radical opposition to the spirit, Paul emphasized the new creation which the coming of the spirit had inaugurated. Whereas the scrolls domiciled the spirit within a legalistic community, this cohabitation was not indicated in the epistles. The seventh chapter of the epistle to the Romans most clearly illustrates the contrast between the flesh and the spirit; in elucidating this antithesis, Paul took a giant step forward in his understanding of the law.

The Antilogy of Life and Death

Flesh and spirit, as Paul understood them, led respectively to death and to life. The term "death" signified spiritual death (sin), bodily death (its consequence), and eternal

---

[13] In the passages cited in this chapter the term "flesh" seems to have a primarily moral connotation.

death (its end); "life" referred to natural life, the life of grace, and the eternal life in which grace attains maturity. When one considers the breadth of meaning encompassed by this antithesis and takes cognizance of the fact that Paul works out the contrast on an extensive rather than an intensive basis, it is easy to understand why the contradistinction resists close analysis. Nevertheless, because this contrast is so intimately connected with Paul's understanding of the law, some attention should be given to it.

Galatians 3:13–14: Emphasis on Death

Only one side of the contrast appears in this passage, but Christ's death is shown as completely shifting men's thoughts away from the prospect of justification through legal observance. The gentiles were condemned by the law because they were strangers to the covenant; the Jews were judged because they failed to obey the terms of the covenant. The law, therefore, brought death to both Jew and gentile.

A curse excluded a man from the covenant community and eventually destroyed life. In freeing man from the curse of death, Christ secured the blessing of life for him. Christ is the very embodiment of the freedom which is life; yet he became the curse which is death so that man might receive the promise of the spirit which is life.

Although Christ suffered physical dissolution, he did not undergo what the scriptures frequently meant by death: the seal and confirmation of final separation from God. Actually, Christ's physical death was the way to true life, the door of joyous return to his Father.[14]

This passage marks an apex in Paul's thoroughgoing repudiation of the law in the epistle to the Galatians. The theme of life through death which permeates the message at every point is used here to express discontinuity. Paul makes three relevant statements which somehow coalesce into one:

---

[14] Barnabas Ahern, "The Lord's Freedom," *The Way*, 2:3 (July, 1962), 168.

(1) the death of Christ makes salvation available to man; (2) man appropriates salvation by participation in Christ's death; (3) the Christian must die to the flesh to live in the spirit. The passage through death on the part of the individual who belongs to Christ is analogous to the radical discontinuity that Paul perceives between the realm of the law and the realm of grace.[15]

Romans 8:10–13: Emphasis on Life

This aspect of the contrast is enclosed within the antithesis of flesh and spirit. Though man will have to die, thanks to the decision for the spirit and against the flesh, this death will bring life. We must be content to live in the spirit, comforted in advance because the bitterness of death has already been endured and conquered on Golgotha. Over all graves there is the promise that men will live forever by the same spirit who raised Jesus.

The power of the flesh and that of the life-giving spirit are within the bodies of believers. Since God gave to all men the power of resurrection, they are debtors to him to use the gift of life in his service. The Christian stands before a decision with conclusive consequences. He must decide between death and life. If he opts for the life of the flesh, he will die; if he chooses the life of the spirit, he will live, but this life will come only by means of death. Within death the seed of life is contained. Paradox this, but perhaps in the converse lies the deeper mystery.

The preceding portion of this epistle emphasized the opposition between the law of the flesh which brings death and the law of the spirit which brings life (8:6). The problem of the man who comes from the world of the law is perplexing: How does one get from an apparent life in the flesh to a true life in the spirit? The answer is emphatically

---

[15] Holt Graham, "Continuity and Discontinuity in the Thought of St. Paul," *Anglican Theological Review*, 38:2 (April, 1956), 142–143.

stated. The spirit is the way to life; at the same time the spirit is life itself.

Resurrection and life are the mark of the new age, and those who continue to live in the old age live in death. God uses the paradox of the will as he uses the paradox of time to reveal the way in which he works. The paradox of time means that in a certain sense man lives in two ages at once. By faith he lives in the world of the spirit with and in Christ, but in the physical universe man also lives in death. The paradox of the will means that although the hearer can be incorporated in the life-giving humanity of Christ, he can also choose the death-giving life of the flesh.

Since Paul's concept is delicately balanced it is impossible to express it in simple and rigid terms. As there is a certain degree of oneness in death and life, so gospel and law are essentially one. Far from being a mystery still hidden from man, the unity of death and life, of gospel and law, has been manifested in the gracious Word of God whose name is Jesus Christ; by his living out of the death-life paradox Christ gave himself wholly to man and claimed man wholly for himself.

Antithesis of the Letter and the Spirit

It will be noticed that one Pauline antithesis is closely bound up with and often contained within another. The contrast between the spirit and the letter is no exception. An exposition of this antithesis necessarily throws light upon that of life and death; a study of the latter leads inevitably to a deeper understanding of the flesh and the spirit. Taken together, all these contrasts illumine the legal entity. This is one manifestation of Paul's genius.

2 Corinthians 3:6–18: A New Perspective

The antithesis between the law and the gospel, old and new covenants, is here expressed as that between the old letter and the new spirit. The new covenant, that of the spirit, gave life, while the old covenant, that of the letter, brought death.

It is quite possible that in this passage Paul reacted to the sectarian concept of a new covenant which would remain that of the letter. At Qumran the spirit was at the service of the letter; in Paul's thinking the reverse was the rule. When Paul commented on hearers who still had the veil over their faces (3:15), he might have been thinking of those who, like the Essenes and the Jerusalem Church, boasted of belonging to a new covenant. For the truly new covenant consists not in a written code but in the spirit who brings liberty and with it an unveiled face and complete transformation.[16]

While judging the death-dealing letter, Paul extolled the life-giving spirit. With the old law, the letter, Paul contrasted the new, the spirit which acts as an internal vivifying principle. To designate the letter, Paul used a Greek word (*grámma*) which elsewhere denotes the law in a deprecatory sense.[17] It would seem that here the term is used in a pejorative sense also.

The commonly-used English translation "letter" of the Greek term *grámma* does not accurately convey Paul's meaning. In describing the law of Moses as a *grámma*, a written document, which was to be an automatic norm for daily actions, Paul placed the spirit and letter in antilogical relationship.[18]

In Paul's day Judaism had lost the synthesis of word and spirit, and the scriptures had become mere letters. The law had become an end in itself rather than a means to evoke faith in God's grace; false interpretations had rendered the word of God ineffectual. Therefore, Paul rejected the law, yet he observed it. The apparent antinomy can be resolved

---

[16] Sherman B. Johnson, "Paul and the Manual of Discipline," *Harvard Theological Review*, 48:3 (July, 1955), 159.

[17] Bernardin Schneider, "The Meaning of St. Paul's Antithesis 'The Letter and the Spirit,'" *The Catholic Biblical Quarterly*, 15:2 (April, 1953), 201.

[18] C. H. Dodd, *Gospel and Law* (New York: Columbia University Press, 1951), p. 70.

by distinguishing between the Jewish emphasis on the letter
(grámma) and the Christian understanding of the spirit
(pneûma).

Paul discerned two diametrically opposed systems: (1) that
of the flesh which sought justification by a punctilious keeping of the letter of the law, and (2) that of the spirit-inspired
man rescued by Christ from the curse of the law. By letter
(grámma) Paul designated the attitude which hoped for
salvation by law-observance. A pseudo-scientific distinction
between ceremonial law and moral law would lead to the false
conclusion that Paul broke with the one and held to the
other. When Paul broke with the law, he broke with it as a
unit. Because of the complete Christian legal emancipation
Paul had to assert that liberty did not mean license.

Paul's life exemplified his teaching that the believer's
liberty must be conditioned by love if it was to be true Christian freedom. In accord with his teaching, Paul restricted his
own liberty for the sake of his weaker brothers. At Corinth
he abstained from certain practices in deference to a group
of Christians, while for the sake of the Jerusalem Christians
he performed certain actions. In both situations Paul refused
to allow neutral and secondary matters to work havoc in the
Church.

While denouncing those who asserted that the law was
necessary for fellowship in the Church, Paul also tolerated in
Christian love the believers who viewed the law as a necessary way of life for all with a Jewish background. In an effort
to keep gentiles free from the law and also to win Jews over
to the new freedom of the children of God, Paul limited the
very liberty he proclaimed. However, his actions were neither
hypocritical nor inconsistent. Only if Paul had acted in opposition to the principles he preached could he have been
charged with hypocrisy and inconsistency. Actually, Paul held
to great principles with incomparable tenacity. His wide
diversity of practice sprang most naturally from his doctrine
of Christian liberty.

The stress in this passage is upon discontinuity. In explaining the significance of the veil which Moses wore, Paul affirms the superiority of the new convenant. In his polemic against Moses, Paul apparently negates any value of the old covenant; the spirit clearly usurps the letter. However, at a deeper level a real continuity is present. When the veil (of the letter) is taken away, the spirit is revealed. The veil has served its purpose; now Christian life would be dominated by the spirit. The action of Christ's spirit inscribes the divine image upon the man freed from the slavery of the letter.

Romans 2:27–29: Inward Nature of the New Law

Paul's purpose in the second chapter of the letter to the Romans was to demonstrate that just as the gentiles were under the wrath of God because they were sinners, so were the Jews who, despite their privileges, were incapable of fulfilling the law. The stark contrast between the old covenant which touched the flesh only externally and the new covenant which possesses the entire being is here developed by means of the antithesis between the spirit and the letter. Circumcision of the flesh, seal of the former contract, was an external sign wrought according to an external code; circumcision of the heart, on the contrary, is an invisible but nonetheless objective sign imprinted by the spirit. Just as the service of the letter condemns whereas the ministry of the spirit justifies (cf. 2 Cor 3:6, 9), so circumsion by the letter is the instrument and seal of condemnation; circumcision in and by the spirit is the instrument and seal of justification.[19]

Four parallel antitheses appear in Romans 2:28–29; one on the name "Jew," two relating to circumcision, and one on the praise merited. Juxtaposed, the elements of the contrast appear:

The Jew who is so outwardly circumcision which is so	The Jew who is so inwardly circumcision (which is so

---

19 Schneider, art. cit., pp. 199–200.

> outwardly in the flesh   inwardly) of the heart
> circumcision by the letter   circumcision in (by) the spirit
> praise from man   praise from God[20]

A close scrutiny of the foregoing parallels reveals a basic consistency underlying the apparent inconsistency. "Jew," "circumsion," and "praise," though with divergent qualifications, appear on both sides of the ledger. When properly understood, circumcision is not merely something external (by the letter); it is an inner reality which is to be accomplished in the spirit.

Severe as these propositions were for the Jews of Paul's time, they are perhaps quite as difficult to comprehend for men of the twentieth century. Only by courageous self-appraisal can a man determine his purity of heart and the authenticity of his service. Beneath the circumcision of the letter the authentic descendant of Judah will experience the more basic circumsion in the spirit.

Romans 7:6: Living Freedom versus Dead Slavery

In this verse where the letter-spirit (grámma-pneûma) antithesis occurs for the third and last time in the writings of Paul, the association of the letter with the law of Moses is unmistakable. Although Paul did not differentiate between moral and ritual laws, it would appear that here the character of law as a moral code is uppermost in his mind.

The identity of concept between the first (2 Cor 3:6) and the last (Rom 7:6) occurrence of this antithesis is so striking that a real parallelism between the two can be postulated. However, here (7:6) instead of the law being removed, man is said to be removed from the law. In each case the result is the same: by dying, freedom to serve in a new spirit is obtained. Freedom is the essential point in this verse. But the biblical concept of freedom never means that man is his own master; rather, it connotes a situation in which man is free to serve God.

---

[20] Ibid., p. 200.

Although Paul was capable of brief, illuminating metaphors, he lacked the gift for sustained illustration of ideas through concrete images. The allegory of slavery is no exception. Although the idea recurs apparently without pattern, each recurrence yields a deeper insight into the basic reality. The present statement of a new type of slavery to be lived not under a written code, but in the spirit, is a rather concise summary of the Pauline message. Touchstone of Paul's moral teaching, the antithesis of letter and spirit graphically illustrates the continuity and also the discontinuity of the legal entity.

The Slavery which Frees

Paul used the category of law to refer to the moral will of God which man is free to make his own but which he cannot change. Paul's concern with ethics and morality as well as his repudiation of the antinomian tendencies of some of his Galatian followers show that he recognized the objective structure of the moral order with which man must come to terms to achieve true freedom. Only by subjecting himself absolutely to Christ can man find freedom. Paradoxically, this freedom flows from a new kind of slavery.

The allegory in Galatians 4:21–31 supports the thesis that the way of the law is the way of enslavement, and the way of faith is the way of freedom. Various elements drawn from the Genesis account suggest the contrast between those who follow the way of the law and those who follow the way of faith. Just as one of Abraham's sons was born into slavery, so the Jews of Paul's day existed in a condition of slavery. As Abraham's son by the free woman inherited freedom, so the children of the heavenly Jerusalem were born free men.

Paul employed analogical material loosely, drawing from it only those elements which would reinforce the point with which he was dealing. In this instance he was primarily interested in showing the discontinuity between the old law and the new law. This preoccupation accounts for fragmentary applications as well as sudden shifts in the comparisons. Paul contended that Jewish legalism was a kind of slavery to which the Galatians should not be subjected; hence he was most interested in showing that the tension between freedom and slavery could be observed in scripture.

Perhaps the most enigmatic statement of this new slavery occurs in Romans 6:15–23. Although the picture is not drawn in detail, enough appears to indicate that Paul was thinking of slavery as a condition in which the submission and obedience of slave to master is a central consideration. The dominance of the idea of obedience is also seen in the rather surprising antithesis of sin and obedience (7:16). The second member of the antithesis is introduced to support the principal idea, namely, that servitude to sin and to obedience are mutually exclusive. In this instance Paul used the analogy of slavery for the idea of exclusive obedience that the illustration suggested; the image should not be applied to all aspects of his religious thinking.

The analogy of slavery can be used as a basis for understanding Paul's thought only within the limits imposed by the context. The latter introduces an anomalous ingredient. The concept of a slavery that is free startles the reader; however, one of Paul's most ingenious devices for imparting supernatural realities lay precisely in injecting paradoxical statements at the most unforseen junctures.

Paul assumed that men would be slaves and, therefore, obedient to some master. Incapable of throwing off some form of servitude, man could only alternate between sin and rightdoing. Paradoxically enough, in expounding the slavery of the Christian, Paul's true concern was to affirm that the Christian situation, far from being one of slavery, is one of freedom in spirit and sonship.

. Laboriously constructed and inconsistent in details, the example nevertheless effectively conveys the basic message: the obvious divergencies between the state of man under the old law and under the new law partly conceal but also strikingly manifest an underlying continuity.

Development of Primitive Moral Catechetical Tradition

To a certain extent the early Jerusalem disciples realized that they were freed from the law. Relying for salvation on what Christ had done for them rather than on their observance of the law, the disciples acted in some degree as free men. Apparently, however, they did not know exactly why they were free nor did they act in accordance with all the ramifications of this freedom.

According to Acts, the case of Cornelius was exceptional; by direct command of the spirit Cornelius had been received into the Church without being circumcised. But most of the early Christians continued to live outwardly in the ordinary Jewish way while inwardly they wrestled with the problem of the law. Thus the freedom of the early Jerusalem Church was held by precarious tenure until its underlying principles were established. Christianity needed theology. And the first Christian theologian was Paul.

Although a certain development of the primitive moral catechetical tradition is discernible in Paul's writings, he certainly did not add new doctrines to the pristine heritage. Rather, this man of intuitive genius altered the lights in which he placed the Christian moral teaching and emphasized aspects which led Christians to a more profound understanding of their new freedom. Paul was original, but it was not his own discovery or invention about which he wrote with such creative power. While taking over the common and apostolic tradition from those who were in Christ before him, Paul also took what was best in the pagan ethic of the time and built thereon the structure of the raw ethical inheritance in Christ. Subtly, but nonetheless clearly, an antithetic flavor pervades the Pauline development of the early moral catechetical tradition.

The End of the Law

An antithetic base is discernible in Paul's statement that Christ is the end (*télos*) of the law (Rom 10:4). This is a key verse for an understanding of Paul's attitude to the law; at the same time the very ambiguity of the verse indicates a certain progression in the primitive moral teaching. Those who emphasize the negative aspect of Paul's attitude toward the law are likely to choose the meaning "termination" from the many possible for the word *télos*. However, if one chooses "goal" as a translation for *télos*, quite a different aura surrounds the verse. In the latter instance a positive connotation replaces the former negative implication.

Although various nuances inhere in the English word "end," the term "goal" seems to convey more of an idea of positive fulfillment. The law was fulfilled in Jesus Christ. Whereas in the Old Testament, the torah was described as the way, in the New Testament the One who fulfilled the law could assert, "I am the way." A law replaced yet continued: this is the paradox presented by Paul in Romans 10:4. Life in Christ became the antithesis of life under the old order.

The Christian Dynamic

The followers of Jesus had received from him a new approach to the moral problems of the time. As a consequence of Jesus' teaching his followers could no longer formulate their ideas of ethical responsibility solely upon the nomistic tradition of Judaism; they were forced to turn to the new ethical life of the spirit. This life produced a greater freedom and creativity than the nomistic tradition allowed. The life in the spirit gave the Church a desire to transform the human situation rather than to withdraw from it. However, this change in outlook did not occur automatically; the transition could only be difficult.

After Paul brought the good news to the gentiles, the Jewish ethical tradition which Christianity had largely assumed was no longer an adequate conveyor of the new moral life. The theological and moral problems which emerged in Paul's churches impelled the apostle to probe the relevancy of old legal traditions. The result was a new expression of Christian freedom from the law.

However, Paul soon discovered that antinomianism and legalism could make strange bedfellows. In his efforts to maintain a nice balance and to interpret legal obligations in a Christian context, Paul must have seemed to Jewish Christians an antinomianist, whereas to the gentile churches he must have appeared as a confirmed moralist. In point of fact, however, Paul was neither. Apostle of freedom though he was, Paul was pre-eminently a catechist whose prophetic concern was to prepare the coming together of God and man. Understanding the Graeco-Roman world and yet rooted in Judaism, Paul was able to transmit a Palestinian gospel to an alien world and yet keep it true to its origins. To maintain these origins while adapting the concepts to the unique situation required delicacy of balance. By using antithesis as a vehicle for his thought, Paul was able to achieve an accurate and yet nonconfining synthetic presentation of the Christian legal entity.

Under Paul's pen dead dilemmas became living paradoxes. The conflict, the tension, the confrontation which ensued brought transforming insights which communicated God's word with a unique relevancy. Basic fulfillment transmitted by apparent repudiation: this Paul achieved by the use of antithesis.

CHAPTER II

TRIPARTITE CHRISTIAN LAW

The New Law

In the Christian paschal mystery a new race of men was born. This lineage inaugurated a new era; in this aeon a new morality came into being.

Greeks and Jews had their own moral laws; that of the Greeks was dictated by reason, and that of the Jews was imposed by God on Mt. Sinai. Greek morality was humanistic; it sought perfection in the order of reason. The Greek sought freedom by subjecting himself to the order of reason for he believed that to obey the eternal laws of nature was merely to be subject to oneself. The possibility of becoming free by opening himself to a totally Other never occurred to him. Because he really did not renounce self the Greek was imprisoned in the laws of this world.

Although assuredly not unreasonable, the morality of the Jew was not of the order of reason. The Jew recognized the precepts of the natural law, but these imperatives received new emphasis from their imposition by God. The whole of Jewish law derived from Sinai. Obedience to Yahweh was the principle of all Jewish wisdom.

From one point of view, Jewish morality was inferior to that of the Greeks. Whereas the Greek recognized only an inward moral imperative, the Jew was bound by an exterior law, a commandment from Yahweh. St. Paul referred to the Jewish law as servile; the Jew was God's slave.

Identical neither with the natural law of the Greek nor with the sinaitic law of the Jew, the new Christian law nevertheless demands submission to God. Truly, Christian life in its entirety is a servitude to God and his justice (Rom 6:16–18). In the old era God made known his will through spokesmen; in the new aeon God reveals his law in Christ, and man submits by his life in Christ. Indeed, to Paul, the Christian law is a law only by analogy.

The Christian movement had already developed before Paul's Christian outlook was defined. Before Paul's apostolate began, disciples like Stephen, Barnabas, and the Christians at Antioch had modified the expression of the Christian faith. The diaspora Judaism from which these men came was different from that of Judea and Galilee; it had been infiltrated by elements of the wider hellenistic world and marked by the results of a long defense against this world. Although Christianity was cradled in Judaism and historically was closely related to the hellenistic culture of the first Christian century, it was the sole product of neither; nor was it the result of a simple fusion of the two cultures. The Christian church was indeed a complex reality.

Paul declared that God had initiated the new age by sending forth his son, the new Adam, and through him was now restoring the broken order. The coming of a new order is always, in a certain sense, a fatality for the old order. The gospel, therefore, was both a life-giving and a death-dealing incense (2 Cor 2:15, 16). The new situation had its prototype in the mosaic foundation. Under the old dispensation a veil lay over Israel, a veil now removed in the new covenant which is one of the spirit and of freedom from the law (2 Cor 3:6–18).

The chief difficulty in understanding Paul's teaching on the law is not the special categories which he used to express his thought; it is rather the level on which his thought moved. Paul dealt with ultimates, and only those who seek answers regarding ultimates will be able properly to evaluate his teaching. The plodding pedestrian who merely literalizes will never come to grips with the continuity of the old law, a continuity which is masked by a real, though surface, discontinuity. The paradox of scripture must be resolved on a higher level than human understanding (Rom 11:33). Only the man who is willing to probe the deeply spiritual will attain a progressive comprehension of the divine mysteries. Not the least among these mysteries is the opposition between spirit and law. This opposition is resolved in a transcending of the law which is fulfillment, not abolition.

Paul certainly was not a systematic theologian. No system ever could have satisfied his untrammelled spirit. Much of his phraseology was fluid; assuredly, it was never rigid. For example, the term "law" can be found in a variety of meanings in his epistles. Paul wrote of the law in lofty, almost exaggerated terms. He seemed to connect the law with sonship, the covenant, and the promises (Rom 9:4). But in another connection Paul apparently affirmed the opposite: " . . . the very commandment which promised life proved to be death to me" (Rom 7:10). Although Paul treated as absurd the idea that the law could be sinful, he discerned a very close connection between the law of God and the sin of man (Gal 3:19; Rom 3:20). Most frequently Paul emphasized the latter aspect when treating of the law.

On occasion, he could regard the law as holy and take genuine delight in it (Rom 7:12, 22); however, quite another aspect of *nómos* impelled him to refer to the curse of the law (Gal 3:13). Obviously, the construction of a doctrinal system was not Paul's aim; more vital, more urgent issues were at stake. In Paul's mind all was subordinate to his one great task. To give resolute witness to the Christian gospel: this was his highest prerogative.

Although he did not formulate a system of ethics, Paul's gospel was ethical to the core. He promulgated no code, nor did he make a scientific classification of virtues. However, for him, religion necessarily implied a morally strenuous and elevated life.

Paul was nurtured in a Jewish environment that had strong hellenistic overtones. He studied under Gamaliel, a grandson of the great Hillel, who represented Pharisaism at its best. Between the school of Hillel, where a more liberal Judaism was inculcated, and the school of Shammai, where an unyielding literalism was taught, constant rivalry prevailed. Proselytes from other faiths were welcomed by Hillel's followers, but the disciples of Shammai barred them altogether. Sitting at the feet of Gamaliel, Paul, undoubtedly, was in touch with the best in the religious education of his people. Yet, the essential characteristics of Pharisaism — its externalizing of man's duty to God, its legal notions of the relation between the human and the divine, its inner hardness — these left their impression on the young hellenistic Jew.

Paul brought with him into Christianity a Jewish interest in the combination of ethics and religion. Since the function of the torah was to produce a holy people, religion and ethics could not be separated. By fulfilling the commands of the law, each religious act of Old Testament man assumed a certain ethical character.

When Paul referred to the new law which was henceforth to be the guiding norm for the Christian, he also pointed to the spirit which would be its motivating force. Expressing a new experience in terms of an old category can be dangerous. While using the old category of law to describe what would henceforth bind Christians, Paul injected a new element. Henceforth, the spirit would be the motivating force for the Christian. The new creation in Christ Jesus would be accomplished by the power of the spirit. To the category of law Paul added his original conception of the community as composed of spirit-guided individuals. Thus the new law was an inner dynamism whose motive force was the spirit of God.

It is not surprising, therefore, to find that Paul identifies the spirit with life (Rom 8:10). In contrast to the debility of the old law, the law of the spirit itself gives the power which enables man to live the Christian life. The spirit is at once the source and sustainer of life in the fully Christian sense.

Paul's concept of the living Christ was so closely connected with his idea of the Holy Spirit that he seemed on occasion to use the two names almost interchangeably. This does not mean that Christ and the spirit are simply identified. The spirit makes Christ real to man and mediates Christ's gifts to him. So close are the ideas of Christ and the spirit in Paul's mind that he can pass almost without a sense of distinction from one to the other. For Paul, to live in the spirit was to live in the presence of the risen Lord. In a very real sense the spirit was the fulfillment of Christ's promise that he would be with Christians even to the end of the world.

Twice Paul referred to the law of Christ (Gal 6:2; 1 Cor 9:19–23), thereby implicitly suggesting that the moral precepts which regulate Christian living still have some of the characteristics of law. Paul certainly did not mean that Christ had laid down a systematic code of laws; he realized that every attempt to formulate detailed rules from the gospel teaching would be doomed to failure. Rather, he provided vivid, occasional glimpses of what the law of Christ demands; this he did in such a paradoxical way that not even the most literal-minded disciple would be able to reduce them to a set of rules. Paul wanted to emphasize the fact that the new law is not an ordinary law; because it is a law of the spirit, it regulates the inner workings of the heart. The lustful look, the gust of anger, violate the interior law which binds the Christian. Ordinary laws can judge only external actions.

Paul defines the new morality as the law of the spirit (Rom 8:2). This means that Christians depend solely on

the Holy Spirit for impulse and inspiration. In the language
of the New Testament, the word "spirit" implies an immanent and dynamic agent. Since the Holy Spirit is the
immediate life-giving principle of the moral life, the Christian
is constantly fortified by his power. "For all who are led
by the spirit of God are sons of God" (Rom 8:14): this is
the hallmark of the Christian. It is because the Christian
renders service to God which is new and according to the
spirit (Rom 7:6) that the economy of the new alliance is
uniquely different from that of the old.

However, the law, the good gift of God, was not simply
rejected when the old covenant was fulfilled; the law was
taken up into the new covenant and finds a new value in it.
Now the old law has been transformed into the law of love.

Only if man views the law within the framework of
covenant, and ultimately of election, will he properly comprehend it. When God has communicated with men in
terms of covenant, a certain unity of conception has prevailed. Always, divine covenants have been revealed as sovereign administrations of grace and promise which were specifically redemptive. Successive covenants were coeval and
correlative with successive epochs in the accomplishment of
God's redemptive will. More, the covenants were themselves
constitutive of these epochs so that redemptive accomplishment became identical with covenant fulfillment. The character of law is determined by covenant, by the proclamation
of the will of God that sets man free. The law simply clari-
fies the significance of the covenant.

In the New Testament epoch when the apex of covenant
administration is reached, sovereign grace and promise are
dispensed on the highest level. Progressive covenant revelation has culminated in the new covenant which brought
with it a new law. Not wholly diverse in principle and character from the old covenant and law, the new covenant and
law are a complete realization of the grace which was the
constitutive principle of all covenants. The new covenant and

law differ from their antecedents in that they bring to fruition the divine-human relationship epitomized in those preceding.) The new covenant is everlasting; it brooks no substantial change. An ultimate reality and yet one that leads ever on to new things: this is the mystery of the new law.

The Enigma of the Christian Law

Paul's writing was full of paradoxes. By habitually offering pairs of ideas which seemed to contradict each other, yet both of which were true, he showed that God did not weigh things according to human standards. The truths which Paul conveyed were too big for human comprehension. To express these truths, he had to speak in contraries.

Perhaps nowhere in his writings did the principle of truth-by-contraries apply with such force as when he wrote about the law. Emphatically, Paul declared that Christians were not under the law, but with like emphasis he affirmed that the law of Christ obliged all Christians. Neither the nature of the law nor the new Christian situation can explain fully the ambiguity of Paul's legal polemic. It would seem that a turbulence deep within him was a partial cause for his difficulty in arriving at a synthesis. Paul's problem stemmed initially from his love for the law. Had he not revered it, he might have slighted it as did some Jews who were influenced by gentile civilization. To the end of his life Paul insisted that the law was holy and good. When his opponents charged that he had set the law aside, Paul hotly denied it (Rom 3:31; 7:1). For Paul, the law remained the utterance of God himself, the standard by which a man's moral deeds were to be measured.

Nevertheless, Paul was apprehensive lest the gospel be transformed into a code. He was aware of the subtle tendency, experienced by devout converts from Judaism, to absorb, depress, and neutralize the gospel by interpreting it in terms of their mature religious institution, the law. However, this

tendency was not peculiar to Jewish converts. Human nature
strains to control the mystery, resolve the paradox, and reduce to quiet normalcy the enigma of a new law which
simultaneously frees and binds. The result of such striving
was to identify the process of sanctification with deeds done
in conformity with a code. Actually, this would mean that
man relied on human activity as the sole source of salvation;
God's free grace would be submerged within a legal system.

Paul accurately assessed the situation and fought the tendency with every resource he could muster. The epistle to
the Galatians is Paul's fiery defense of true Christian spirituality, his most vigorous rejection of human activity as the
sole principle of salvation. A master-idea of Galatians — man
is made holy not merely by literal observance of law — is
stated emphatically in 2:16. Although it would be unwise to
take what Paul wrote in Galatians, because of the polemical
character of this epistle, as a starting point in an understanding of his teaching on the law, investigation reveals
that the same idea permeates the more irenic presentation
in the epistle to the Romans. In Rom 3:21–24, for example,
Paul uses the analogy of Jewish legal religion to describe
what is inexplicable in literal terms: that God accomplishes
man's salvation in Christ.

In his wrestlings with the problem of the law, Paul came
to realize that the reconciliation of the world to God in
Christ meant that the principle of law had been replaced
by that of love. The Christian law meant the abandonment
of all the basic principles of legalism in man's relations
with God, for the essence of such legalism is the belief
that man's achievement is the basis of his standing in the
sight of God. Such a religion moves exclusively in the sphere
of commandments and prohibitions, duty and transgressions,
merit and guilt, reward and punishment. Paul realized that
the act of God in Christ had taken man's relationship to

God out of this area; in the new era the relationship was based solely on love.[1] Chapters Twelve and Thirteen of the epistle to the Romans contain the fullest exposition of the conduct of the new man in Christ. The basic rule of the new ethic — that the Christian's conduct must be different because of what God has done in Christ — is stated in 12:1–2. Paul's ethic is one of love. In the new era love is the bond that unites all members of Christ and makes all serve the others; this is the fruit of the spirit. Love is above the law. The law of Christ, however, is a law of love. Basically, this is the enigma of the Christian law.

The promptings of the Holy Spirit constitute the law of Christ. This new law is an interior dynamism which makes the Christian able to perceive the supernatural meaning of his existence so that he is no longer satisfied with the minimum requirements of an external law. Rather, while living God's own life, the new man in Christ responds to the impulses of divine grace.

However, for the present, the Christian lives in the state of tension of the time in between. Paul depicts this situation by describing the two ages (Rom 5). The age of Adam is one of sin, law, and death; the era of Christ is the dispensation of grace, righteousness, and life. Although the Christian continues to exist in the old aeon, he also lives in the new age, for he belongs to the body of Christ and participates in the eschatological community. In this time when the old age and the new era overlap the Christian life is one of constant struggle.

An ethic based on love is harder to observe than a rigid system of rules which prescribe performance for each ethical situation. The Christian ethic takes cognizance of the unique demands of each situation; the principle of love relates to

---

[1] C. W. H. Lampe, "The Atonement: Law and Love" *Soundings: Essays Concerning Christian Understanding*, ed. A. R. Vidler (Cambridge: University Press, 1962), p. 178.

different situations in varying ways. Moreover, each situation has moral demands, and every response has ethical implications. Thus, the man of faith must endeavor to respond to the love of God according to the law of his inner being. The law of the spirit does not differ from the torah merely because it proposes a higher ideal and imposes greater demands. Neither does the new law replace the yoke of the old law with one that is easier to bear. The new law differs radically from the old. It is not an external norm of action; it is a new inner source of spiritual energy.[2]

Ideally, the new man in Christ does not require an external law to constrain him; led by the spirit he fulfills every law in perfect freedom. However, as long as he remains on earth, the Christian possesses the spirit only imperfectly (see Rom 8:23; 2 Cor 1:22). In this situation the external law expresses the inner law. Since the safeguarding of the Christian's inner dynamism is the sole aim of external law, it derives its value from this dynamism and not the other way around. While not neglecting the letter, the Christian is more concerned with the spirit; he views the law as a concretizing of the inner promptings of the spirit. Not presuming to understand fully the enigma of a Christian law, the new man in Christ can acknowledge the mystery while at the same time he appreciates the existential necessity of law.

Faith, the Foundation of Christian Existence

Fidelity is the aspect of faith most emphasized in the Old Testament; references to faith as belief are rare. Although the concept of faith as belief developed in the Christian dispensation, a certain continuity with the Old Testament emphasis perdured.

In the Christian era, however, faith was given a new

---

[2] Stanislas Lyonnet, "St. Paul: Liberty and Law," The Bridge, IV, ed. John M. Oesterreicher (New York: Pantheon Books, 1962), 240.

Person upon whom to rest. Paul emphasized the fact that now faithfulness to God could no longer be practiced apart from faith in Christ, son of God and savior of the world. In the New Testament era the idea of faith as belief complements the pristine idea of faith as fidelity.[3] It should be noted, however, that for Paul faith is primarily belief in a person; it is not the intellectual acceptance of a body of doctrines.

Although the new law is a unity, it is a threefold reality. Faith, hope, and love are not identical; they reveal in different ways the working of the new law. Paul taught that faith is the vital Christian principle, the base upon which the Christian structure rests.

Triple Aspect of Faith

A term with such a rich religious content is not easy to define, and Paul attempted no definition of faith. However, three aspects of faith in Paul's letters approximate an identification of the reality. For Paul, faith is, first of all, a relationship of fidelity; on the natural level, this usage would

---

[3] In *The Semantics of Biblical Language* (London: Oxford University Press, 1962), pp. 201–203, James Barr remarks that the fact that Hebrew usage had developed no substantive equivalent to the Greek *pístis* should not be explained from a total theological structure; it is a simple linguistic fact. The Greek word enriched the lexical stock by providing a semantic marker for the Jewish tradition of belief which in the Old Testament was available in verbal but not in nominal form. Barr regards it as fortunate that Paul had at his disposal a word for trust and believing in the syntactically convenient noun form.

However, it would seem that Gerard S. Sloyan, "Faith and Modern Subjective Thought," *Proceedings of the Eighteenth Annual Convention of the Catholic Theological Society of America* (New York: The Catholic Theological Society of America, 1964), p. 78, comes closer to an exact delineation of the theological significance of the term when he says: "It is not true to say, as Buber says, that the former *emuna* is the sole type of faith known to Israel as a believing community, and that *pístis* represents the incursion of a hellenist idea into late Judaism, namely assent by individuals to the truth of propositions that on the face of them are absurd, even contradictory to the biblical or Jewish mentality. These two types of faith are not mutually exclusive but are two sides of the same coin. Better still, there is faith taken generically — confidence, trust in God — one aspect of which, belief in the truth of God's word, comes into focus as a special type of the exercise of that trust."

connote faithfulness. In Gal 5:22 faith is simply the loyalty
which is one of the most valued qualities to be sought in
a friend. Likewise, when Paul writes that the faith of the
Roman church is spoken of throughout the world, the reference is again to fidelity. In the epistle to the Romans (3:3)
Paul contrasts the faithlessness of Israel with the fidelity
of God. The term has the same meaning of fidelity in 1 Th
3:6 where Paul states that he has received the good news
of their faith. In its most elemental aspect, then, faith is
unshakable loyalty to Jesus Christ.

Closely connected with the first aspect in Paul's letters
is that of faith as belief in Christ as son of God and savior.
In 1 Cor 2:5 Paul admonishes the Corinthians not to let
their faith stand on wisdom. The meaning here is that their
conviction that Christ is the Lord should not be dependent
upon human reasonings. In 1 Cor 15:17 Paul bases faith
unalterably on the risen Christ. *therefore people who*

Quite often in Paul's writings faith stands for the Christian religion. Christianity is *the faith*. For example, in the
epistle to the Galatians (1:23) Paul states that the Palestinian
Christians were bewildered that he was preaching the faith
against which he had once fought so vigorously. In the letter
to the Colossians (1:23; 2:7) as well as in those to the
Corinthians (1 Cor 16:13; 2 Cor 13:5) the term "faith"
also means the Christian religion. However, the very use
of the word in these instances is suggestive; Christianity is
not a system; it is a faith. And the moving force of Christianity is the dynamism of personal faith in Jesus Christ.

Stages of Faith

Perhaps even more important than the foregoing consideration of the senses in which Paul uses the term faith is the
identification of three stages in the Christian act of faith.

For Paul who placed the concept of *pístis* in the center of
his theology, faith is first the acceptance of the kerygma.
Faith is receptivity; the whole epistle to the Galatians attacks

the misunderstanding that faith would have to be supplemented by the performing of works of the law. Although faith is the complete surrender of a man to God, this surrender is basically free, willed decision. Faith is, therefore, an act in which the whole man is involved, while in the case of works, man always stands beside what he accomplishes. The active nature of man's openness which is faith is difficult to express in human language.

From receiving the gospel, man progresses to assent; he assents, not merely to the facts, but to the significance of the facts. The one great fact that includes all others is that the word of God, Jesus Christ, is the saving act of God. Faith is a being seized by Christ (Phil 3:12), allowing the act of salvation to happen to oneself (Col 1:13); it is a decision for God.

Finally, man passes from assent to a realization of the divine love which calls. This realization impels man to respond in faith to love. The response is one of submission to the sovereign will of God. The response of obedience inaugurates the Christian life, and its unfolding is no more than a submission to God, to Christ, to the gospel. Overtones of obedience are frequently evident in Pauline usage. For example, Rom 1:8 which extols the faith of the Roman Christians is paralleled by Rom 16:19 which recounts the fame of their obedience. The total assent of a man's whole being to Christ: this is the culmination of faith.

Man is capable of active orientation to God only to the extent that he is passive in the presence of the divinity. The unique combination of passive activity is a guiding thought underlying many Pauline formulations (see 1 Cor 8:3; 13:2; Gal 4:9; Phil 3:12). Faith finds true actualization only in love[4] (Gal 5:6). Thus, the ethic of faith expresses itself in love. Faith includes the reality of love toward God, but

---

[4] Gottfried Quell and Ethelbert Stauffer, "ἀγαπάω, ἀγάπη, ἀγαπητός," Theological Dictionary of the New Testament, I, ed. Gerhard Kittel, trans. Geoffrey Bromiley (Grand Rapids: Wm. B. Eerdmans Publishing Company, 1964), 50.

it is a love of which the keynote is receptivity, not spontaneity. In its essence the Christian way of life is an answer in faith and love to the divine call.

Love, New Testament Law of Morality

The life to which God invites men is one of love. When Christ freed man from the law, he also freed man for the law. He freed man for the life of love, a life which fulfills the law (Rom 13:10).

The law of love, which is the law of Christ, is no superimposed command. It is the law of man's life; it is the voice of eternity in man's heart. The law of love is part of the evidence, present in man's being, that man is subject to a more exacting demand than any human tribunal can impose or human effort can fulfill. The law which man obeys is one that emanates from his deepest being. Having received God's love, the Christian is constrained to act in love.

God's Active Love

Paul seldom used the word "love" with God as its object. He preferred to think of God as the agent and man as the recipient of divine love through Christ. In two of the three instances where Paul referred to man's love for God, he reversed man's position before the end of the sentence (see 1 Cor 8:3; Rom 8:28). Although Paul thought of man as having an obligation of reverence, devotion, and obedience to God, he did not use the term "love" to describe it. He customarily thought of God as the source of love, not its object. Men were regarded as recipients of love, not its givers. Paul habitually used the word "faith" to designate man's response to God's love.

The love of which Paul writes is not merely an attitude of God toward man; it is not a fact about God in which men profess belief. Rather, love is the very reality of God coming to man; it is the substance of God's life being given to man. Love is not an attribute of the person; it is the person himself going out, giving himself, to another.

Specifically, the love of which Paul wrote was God's own love as it came to man in the whole event of Christ's life, death, and resurrection. Abstract terms are inadequate to describe the reality; its distinctive nature is indefinable. Definition places limits, and it is impossible to delimit God's love. It may be apprehended but not comprehended; it may be exemplified but not exhausted. The nearest human terms can come to describing the entity is by referring to it as God's love in Christ.

The true meaning of *agápē* cannot be expressed; it can only be experienced. When man experiences the love of God reaching out to him, he is impelled to respond in faith to God and in love toward men. Thus, through faith love dwells in man as the controlling force of ethical action, and God's love initiates and sustains both man's faith and his love.

Because Paul thought of love as both the spring and controlling force for Christian moral conduct, he set love sharply against the law and trusted Christians to live freely in love. Having his ethical standard within himself, the Christian is morally autonomous. He is free from external coercion, but the reign of the spirit of Christ is far more demanding than any code. God's active love brooks no mediocrity; it will rest only when all is transformed in Christ Jesus.

When Paul referred to love as the fulfillment of the law (Rom 13:10), he used *agápē* to designate the unique character of God's love. *Agápē* was used only infrequently in classical Greek literature. It was a colorless word which had few associations. The fact that it had hitherto been a cold term enabled the Christians to endow it with their own warmth. Christian literature first gave the noun real currency.

Whereas *éros* and *philía* were commonly used to designate love, Paul and the early Christians chose the less familiar *agápē*, giving it a distinctively Christian meaning. Unfortunately, the English word "love" obscures the meaning which agápē conveyed to Paul and the early Christians. The active love which was revealed in the Christ-event and which provided the Christian dynamic — primarily Paul meant this when he used the word agápē.

Human Consequences of Divine Love

The consequence of divine love and at the same time the characteristic mark of the Christian is love for others. Paul describes this love as one which goes out to all men. Responding to the Father's love, the Christian works toward divine universalism in his relations with his fellowmen. His Christian love is not only a sharing in Christ's love; it is not only Christ loving in him. It is also Christ whom he loves. In going out to others, the Christian goes out to Christ because those others are one with him. A benevolence both disinterested and efficacious, universal and reciprocal: this is the manifestation of God's love in the Christian life.

The reproduction of the divine love by Christians in relationships which involve forbearance is a frequent theme in the Pauline epistles (see Eph 4:32 ff, for example). The charity which Paul urges is the expression of an inward life ruled by the spirit. Men who belong to Christ are expected to live always Christ's death and resurrection which they began to share at baptism. The unselfishness of this living will be manifested in the fruits of the spirit which Paul summarizes in the epistle to the Galatians (5:22–23). In Rom 15:30 Paul implies that the mutual love of Christians should move them to pray for one another. To be united in the death and resurrection of Christ is to vow a most profound attachment to the neighbor (2 Cor 7:3) and to Christ (2 Tim 2:11).

Paul, as well as the other New Testament writers, seemed hesitant to designate as love a benevolence which was shown toward those who would refuse it. Apparently the reason was that for him true charity was a reciprocal love. This reciprocity seemed to be bound up with the efficacy of Christian love. Paul regarded love that was accepted as efficacious and love that was refused as in a certain sense ineffective. Although in some instances the contrary may seem to be true, agápē is essentially an efficacious love. This is the love that God communicates to men in the crucified and risen Christ.

The charity of which Paul wrote in the great hymn of praise to love (1 Cor 13:1–13) was primarily love of neighbor, though Paul could not separate this love from God's love for man and man's response to God's love. After enumerating the characteristics of this love, Paul concluded the delineation by emphasizing its enduring quality. Pressures from the outside notwithstanding, true love remains constant.

The relations between Paul and the church at Corinth illustrate the consequences of Christian love in a community. When Paul visited Corinth, he had been insulted and defied. Instead of returning, he wrote a sharp letter. However, later he explained (2 Cor 2:4) that his severity was inspired by no animosity; it was dictated solely by love. In the next section of the epistle (2 Cor 2:5–11) Paul asked the faithful to reinstate in their love the one who had directly or indirectly caused him such pain. Thus, the forgiving as well as the enduring quality of Christian love was exemplified.

In the hymn of praise to love the emphasis is not upon narrow moral regulations. Upon occasion the latter are likely to absorb completely the Christian's attention. Paul taught that true brotherly love gives the Christian inward freedom from petty preoccupations and exaggerated emphasis on minutiae. In the climax of this section, Paul shows the superiority of charity over all other gifts. Proclaiming the primacy of love, Paul emphasizes the essential aspects of the virtue. It is not merely loyalty to the community that Paul urges: underlying all his counsels on love lies the conception of love as the law of the spirit, a law which stringently binds and expansively liberates the Christian community.

In the epistle to the Romans (13:8–10) Paul insists that love is its own ethic and it requires no supplementing from the Jewish torah or any other code. One can fulfill legal obligations in such a way that he is no longer indebted. However, the Christian can never be free from the responsibility of loving. One always owes love not only because it is practiced imperfectly in this time of tension but also because the will to love is a never-ending movement. Loving as if he could fulfill its highest demands, the Christian will accomplish God's law, given in the Old Testament but valid forever. In one of his finest utterances Paul shows that by a love which manifests itself in a life of active service and devotion to the interests of others the Christian will fulfill the whole law.

Ultimately, the Christian ethic leads back to Christ himself. Christian ethics certainly is not slavish obedience to the law. It is active living and has the power to respond creatively as befits the new man in Christ. But the new creature is still in the process of becoming; he is still straining toward a new order of things. The Christian's active love expresses yet another aspect of his life in Christ. In hope he yearns for the day when his faltering efforts to love shall attain the maturity worthy of the son of God.

Hope, Eschatological Perspective of Christian Liberty

The Christian way of life has a triple dimension. Responding in faith and hope to the divine love, the Christian exults in his divine sonship and voluntarily subjects himself to the spirit that frees him. An indissoluble relationship exists among the three aspects of the Christian law. In faith God bestows upon man a new outlook (Rom 5:2 ff), the assurance of full redemption (Rom 8:38), the expectation of eternal inheritance (Gal 3:29). When faith in Christ looks to the future, it becomes hope. Yet this future is not remote; it is the future of the Lord which is in the process of becoming the present.

Christian hope breaks through time. The Christian cannot passively await his recompense; he must act to attain the glory for which he hopes. But hope is not merely the straining toward a distant event. Mysteriously, but really, hope possesses its object. Certainly, man does not grasp it fully — if so, it would no longer be hope. But even in the present man possesses the germ; he enjoys the firstfruits. Christian hope has a double perspective: it is at once in time and in eternity.

In Christ: Present Perspective of Hope

Paul's moral doctrine has two focal points: the redemption already given in Christ, and the salvation not yet attained toward which man must strive.[5] The phrase "in Christ" occurs more than one hundred sixty times in Paul's letters. It is Paul's favorite way of expressing the most important fact of the Christian existence: in the present era man has already been saved in Christ.

The complexity of the present perspective of Christian hope is difficult to express in human language. However, in the epistle to the Romans (8:24–25) Paul makes a nice distinction between the two aspects of hope. "For in this hope we were saved" (aorist). The past tense used with the concept of hope strikingly portrays the mixed mental attitude toward the idea of salvation. The appended remark, "hope that is seen is not hope," brings the other aspect to the foreground.

Perhaps the most emphatic statement of the present perspective of hope is Rom 13:11. Although the term "hope" does not occur in this passage, Paul here affirms the imminent actuality of the hoped-for salvation with characteristic urgency. Thus Christian hope rests on the acts of salvation accomplished in Christ, and since the act of salvation is eschatological, hope has an inescapable eschatological per-

---

[5] Rudolf Schnackenburg, *The Moral Teaching of the New Testament*, trans. J. Holland-Smith and W. J. O'Hara (New York: Herder and Herder, 1965), p. 278.

spective. The present aeon is the time for confidence.

In the present man is free in Christ. Paul's ethical teaching springs from an inward loyalty to the savior which gives moral discernment and moral power. The new man in Christ is the guarantee of the subjection of all things to God through Christ. To be in Christ is to have the resurrectional power that is given to all those who are in union with him. This power begins to operate in the Christian at the time of his baptism (Rom 6:4–5). The new life in Christ is the guarantee of the fulfillment of eschatological hopes.

In Christ God the Father conceived and accomplished all things. In Christ the Christian has in a certain sense attained his hope. When Paul states that the Christian is in Christ, he implies more than a psychological relationship of knowledge and love; he describes an organic relationship which transforms as it matures. While rejecting the notion of fusion or absorption, the Christian's dawning consciousness of his new status will lead him finally to utter a mysterious "I Am." The phrase "in Christ" describes the nature of Christian man at the most profound level.

The new humanity, although it will be completely formed only in the future, has already come into being. The Church is more than the promise of the new man in Christ; it is the new man existing within history as fully as the limitations of history will permit. The Church is in very truth the presence and being of Christ among us. Now Christ has his being in the community of those who remember him, love him, and hope for his appearing. The memory is a corporate memory, the love a communal devotion, the hope a common hope.

Being in Christ means, even now, a radically different ethical orientation. The law of his inner being impels the man in Christ to open himself to his brothers. The love that is the ground of his hope goes out in abundance to his fellowmen. If faith is the Christian's upward movement, the yielding up of self to God in Christ, hope is his anchor thrown into the heavens, and the motive for his charity (Col 1:5).

With Christ: Future Aspect of Hope

When Paul attempts to explain the state of the Christian in the future, he often uses the same expression; "with Christ" expresses the double idea of proximity and community. The intense hope of being with Christ is the fruit of love; it is the hope of those who aspire to see Christ and enjoy his presence.

The moral life takes its direction from the certitude of this encounter. Convinced that he will see Christ and live with him eternally, the Christian dedicates his whole existence to Christ. Now he realizes that his transformation into Christ will be perfect only in heaven, for "to be with Christ" is not only to see and possess him; it is to have a share in his glory, his fidelity, his reign. It is to be one with Christ.

Inasmuch as Christ's second coming will enable Christians to participate in the divine glory, Christ himself is the object of man's hope. In the measure that men are in Christ they already participate in the kingdom of Christ (Col 1:13), but when Christ is manifested, the new creature will be revealed with him in glory (Col 3:4). This is the term of Christian hope.[6]

Insofar as the Christian lives in time, his existence may be described as a life in hope. In this time hope keeps the Christian in a state of fruitful tension, one in which a desire for eternal life prepares him to receive imperishable blessings. Christian hope is a combination of expectation and patience, of desire and forbearance. The eighth chapter of the epistle to the Romans is permeated with the longing expectation of the revelation of the glory of Christ. This revelation will also be the manifestation of man's hidden glory, of his real life that is already with Christ in God (Col 3:1–3).

---
6 W. Grossouw, "L'Espérance dans le Nouveau Testament," *Revue Biblique*, 61:4 (October, 1954), 524.

The man who looks forward to the time when he will be with Christ lives in a constant and insurmountable tension. His fundamental aspiration toward the risen Christ tends to increase the tension; at the same time, however, the fact that the Christian already lives in Christ alleviates the stringency somewhat. Though basically the Christian looks to the future age for relief from this tension, in the present era the risen Christ can be found in the love of Christians.

Paul's later epistles abound in texts where, with moving and humble simplicity, he avows his impatience to see Christ. However, Paul's hope found expression in the dominant theme of his apostolic dynamism: the passion to serve, born of the passion to love. The Christian who follows Paul's way of alleviating the tension of the time in between will find that he progresses ever more rapidly toward the realization of his hope.

The Holy Spirit, described by Paul as firstfruits and pledge (Rom 8:23; 2 Cor 1:22; 5:5), constitutes the first installment of the eternal life and is proof that the age to come has dawned, although it has not yet been consummated. God who has already given men the spirit may be trusted to give them their full inheritance in due course. Christian hope is grounded in the partial actualization of what it anticipates in fullness. The Christian has a foretaste of his future inheritance. But the very form of man's union with Christ cries out for dissolution and replacement by the full richness of the age to come. This is man's hope, but his hope has already been partially realized. He has died to the old and been raised to the new. Dying, he has risen to a new and better life, and a new and better law guides him on his way to the Father.

Inner Consistency of Paul's View of the Law

The Christian experience of being in Christ and the new ethic are one. The Christian is born into a new life which gives moral emancipation. The new man has his ethical standard within, and that is the real secret of his moral freedom. No longer a slave to external ethical codes, he now submits to an inner law, the law of the spirit (Rom 8:2). Love, the law of the spirit, is the principle which gives expression to the life of God in the Christian community (Col 3:14). But the Christian ethic is more than a law; it is a gospel.

This gospel, this law of the spirit, liberates from the old law, but the deliverance binds man completely to God, to his *agápē*. Whence comes the special dialectic between slavery and freedom in Paul's writings. This dialectic of slavery and freedom is transposed into a dialectic of death and life, of death to the present world, of anticipated entrance into this world of the resurrection. A probing of the consequences of this transposition can lead a man to an ever deepening comprehension of the once-for-all character of the divine legislation.

We cannot move in a straight line from the New Testament to the Christian law. But neither can we live the Christian law without an understanding of the proclamation that lies at the heart of the New Testament. "For I . . . died to the law, that I might live to God. . . . It is no longer I who live, but Christ lives in me; and the life I now live . . . I live by faith in the Son of God" (Gal 2:19–20). This is the core of Christian ethics; this is the *raison d'être* of the Christian law.

The conception of Christ as introducing a new covenant and bringing the definitive law permeates Paul's writings. It is not surprising, therefore, that *nómos* was used in Jewish Christian theology to designate Christ.[7] The personal identification of Christ with the law and the covenant was but the fruition of the deep inner consistency of Paul's presentation of the law. Total expression of man's relation with

---

[7] Jean Daniélou, *The Theology of Jewish Christianity*, trans. and ed. John A. Baker (Chicago: The Henry Regnery Company, 1964), pp. 164–165.

God, Christ is the effective witness of the continuous character of the covenant. Christ, the new law, is the ultimate toward which Paul's writings pointed. Law of Christ, law of love, law of the spirit — there is no distinction. The law of the new era *is* Christ. In a real though less obvious manner he is the law of the old aeon also.

CHAPTER III

ESSENTIAL FREEDOM OF LIFE
IN THE SPIRIT

Background of Paul's Teaching on Freedom

Fluidity of Freedom Concept

The term "liberty" is so porous that interpretations seem to multiply almost automatically. Throughout history men have embraced this concept endowing it with such a varied assortment of connotations that today no standard definition can be expected adequately to represent the term in all contexts. Paul's thought on the subject is quite complex; he does not so much balance the concepts of legality and liberty against each other as measure them both by Christ. His teaching regarding the abrogation of the law and that relative to Christian liberty are intimately related, yet they are distinct.

No man ever fought for freedom as did Paul; freedom was his cry against Jewish legalism. In the letter to the Galatians he pitted freedom against bondage. But it was a particular type of freedom and a special kind of bondage of which he wrote. The freedom was that liberation which came with faith and the spirit; the bondage was that which came with slavery to the letter of the law. The liberation was freedom from the necessity of attaining one's own righteousness, but it was also a liberation to serve in love (Gal 5:14).

Phrygian Galatia was the scene of a decisive battle in the war for Christian freedom. The events which occurred later in Corinth and in Rome were somewhat in the nature of aftermath. The letter to the Galatians, charter of Christian liberty that it was, was not less incisive because of its polemical tone. Although Paul expressed himself so briefly that his allusions were sometimes obscure, the outlining of fundamental ideas clearly revealed the structure of his thought.

Paul's zeal for the law compelled him to speak of freedom as vigorously as he did. Since he had met the risen Christ, Paul had come to a deeper understanding of the law and the precepts which were its application. God had provided a new interpretation of the law which was simultaneously an exposition of the scriptural delineation and a new creation which brought new life. Now a man who would seek righteousness through the works of the law would contend against the deepest meaning and purpose of the law. Paul did not advocate a freedom from the will of God as expressed in the law; rather, he enunciated a liberty which would free man to realize the divine will. When he lived the life of the spirit, the new man in Christ was truly free. But the positive content of this freedom was a relationship to Christ which was also slavery.

Paul taught that the slave of Christ was freed from the obligations of the law. However, he did not advocate Christian anarchy. For Paul the Christian was freed from externally imposed obligations, which have been replaced by another principle of action, the spirit; the Christian lives in Christ, and Christ lives in him. Now the Christian is impelled by an inner power; he does not act because of external compulsion. He can perform only one saving act; this is the saving act of love. Love, far from being merely the fulfillment of an obligation, is a spontaneous movement, the result of the activity of the indwelling spirit.

Baptism empowers the Christian to do that which is impossible for unregenerate man. As long as the Christian does not fully exercise his baptismal power he is not truly free. To a certain extent he is still a slave to the law, and for Paul this is the same as being enslaved by sin. Although the baptismal binding to Christ effectively replaces former ties to sin and to the law, the liberation in the spirit effected by the Christian bond is not yet completed (2 Cor 3:18). At the parousia the union with Christ will be completed, and then the Christian will be fully liberated.

The contrast between the teaching of Paul and that of Epictetus highlights some salient points in Paul's teaching on freedom. Epictetus recommends flight into an inner subjective realm as a means of liberation. Even when man retreats thus, however, he remains a prisoner of his own thoughts and desires. Paul's doctrine of freedom, on the other hand, assures man of eventual liberation from external bonds even while he admits external dependence in the present. The liberty advocated by Epictetus results in the weary lassitude of a man caught as a prisoner by his own ego; the freedom preached by Paul stimulates to the energetic activity of a man who values his Christ-earned freedom. With Epictetus liberty was a laborious process of self-liberation accomplished by prolonged and tortuous reasoning. Paul preached a freedom that results from believing in Christ; faith in Christ frees a man from his ego and effectively binds him to God.

Paul was neither a fanatic torn by extreme tensions nor was he a thinker tortured by the modern distress of existence. He was a man of faith, pressing on to his heavenly Lord with a force born of love. Obviously, faith in Christ does not eliminate the reasoning process. However, Christian freedom rests primarily on faith; it does not result from the reasoning process advocated by Epictetus.

Epictetus emphasized man's struggle for freedom; Paul emphasized God's action in freeing man. Christian liberty is man's freedom to become what he already is in Christ. The freedom which Epictetus advocated is the outcome of a human struggle to become self-sufficient and to gain supreme command over life and death. Christian liberation from sin and from the law includes essentially freedom from the self-deception of the autonomous existence advocated by Epictetus.[1] The difference between these two concepts of freedom is not merely superficial; the opposition is radical. Differences notwithstanding, a consideration of the possible Greek influence upon Paul's delineation of Christian freedom is essential if one would come to an understanding of his thought.

Hellenistic Influence

Tarsus, Paul's native city, had been for a long time an important metropolis in the Greek world. Its intellectual life and the general love of knowledge displayed by its inhabitants attracted students from all parts of the world. It is possible that Paul had some connection with the university of Tarsus; at the very least he came in touch with the doctrinal principles emanating therefrom.

Although it had the characteristics of all seaport towns, Tarsus was permeated by Greek culture and philosophy. The strong oriental element made Tarsus even more pre-eminently a city of culture. But by Paul's time classical Greek culture was no longer extant. The syncretist culture of the Mediterranean where Greek was spoken is now designated as Hellenism. Initiated by the whirlwind conquests of Alexander (334 B.C.–323 B.C.), this dynamic and creative culture took possession of the ancient Near East with a rapidity that was awesome.

Although Jewish communities in Greek cities maintained a certain degree of autonomy, one should not imagine that Jews and gentiles lived wholly apart. A constant borrowing from one another combined with a Jewish elasticity and adaptability resulted in a complexus that was easy to identify but hard to specify.

---

[1] Heinrich Schlier, "ἐλεύθερος," *Theological Dictionary of the New Testament*, II, ed. Gerhard Kittel, trans. Geoffrey Bromiley (Grand Rapids: Wm. B. Eerdmans Publishing Company, 1964), 498.

This complex cultural influence was not confined to the Jews of the dispersion. According to the Talmud (*Sotah* 49b), R. Simeon b. Gamaliel II conducted an academy which featured a dual curriculum: half of the boys studied the wisdom of the Jews while the rest of the student body learned the wisdom of the Greeks. The synagogues of the dispersion customarily invited visitors to participate in their services. When these visitors came from Jerusalem they had to be able to speak in a style which would be acceptable to educated Jews and gentiles alike. Emissaries also needed some knowledge of philosophy, particularly of that mixture of Stoicism and Platonism which was peculiarly congenial to Jewish missionary propaganda; a knowledge of Greek literature was also required background.

Given Greek cultural pre-eminence, it was natural that the rabbis would encourage some of their more promising pupils to study Greek culture. It may be that Paul acquired his formal education in Greek literature and wisdom in this way at the feet of Gamaliel. Even aside from his formal education, it would seem that judaic Hellenism was a factor of some consequence in the background of this Pharisee of the diaspora. Although primary sources are lacking for the Jewish community or Tarsus at this time, it is probable that this community experienced religious, social, and philosophical impacts similar to those felt by the Jews of Alexandria. Hence it seems legitimate to suppose that hellenistic elements of culture were assimilated by the Jews of Tarsus; unless a diaspora community is artificially confined to a ghetto, such a process of assimilation is inescapable. That Paul was influenced by the religion of his fathers and also by the religious movements of the hellenistic world of his day is undeniable. However, the extent to which he was indebted to the one or to the other will probably always be a matter of conjecture; in the fusions of the first Christian century it is impossible accurately to separate hellenistic, judaic, and other multiple factors.

Not the least significant among the cultural factors was that of language. The Jews outside Palestine wrote and generally thought in Greek. Presumably, Greek was Paul's native tongue; so far as we know, Greek was the exclusive medium for his literary efforts. As could be expected, therefore, he also employed Greek forms of expression in his epistles. When Paul wrote of freedom, there was a certain similarity with the mode of expression of the Stoics. For example, the Greek citizen was considered free because he obeyed no other man; but he was a slave in the same measure that he was free. Liberty implied the taking part in public activities; in the public assembly he participated in making the law. Therefore, when he obeyed the law he obeyed himself.[2] For the Greek, freedom was man's ultimate goal.

Paul also wrote of a freedom that implied obedience. In fact, he sometimes affirmed Christian liberty and slavery in the same sentence. However, Paul never preached freedom as the ultimate goal toward which all human effort should be directed. He deemed Christian freedom to be such a reality that he did not consider the bodily emancipation of the slave to be important. What was important had been accomplished in Christ; the Christian slave was a freedman of the Lord, while he who was free when called became a slave of Christ (1 Cor 7:20–22).

The comparative lack of interest in the social fact of slavery shown by the writers of the New Testament is not due primarily to the eschatological tension of early Christian life. Rather, it is based on the redeeming act of Jesus which applies to all men irrespective of status and origin because all have equal need of it. The act of Christ, however, acquires significance for the individual only within the concrete relationships in which he lives, because it is only within these that he commits sin. In the New Testament sin always takes the form of concrete disobedience to God; hence the

---

[2] Andre Festugüre, *Liberté et Civilisation chez les Grecs* (Paris: Éditions de la Revue des Jeunes, 1947), pp. 31–32.

goal of the New Testament proclamation is the control of the situation of the individual by the act of Jesus, so that the Christian can produce an attitude and action which are conformable to this act. Therefore, the primary goal of the slave won for Christ is not the attainment of freedom; it is that as a slave he should live unto the Lord.[3]

Freedom is never demanded but is to be gratefully received whenever possible. External freedom is valuable. Its value is only relative, however, when compared with the freedom for God and his will which is the gift of Christ. Indeed, when Christian freedom is taken seriously it presupposes a self-dedication which not all Christians are either prepared or able to accept.

New Testament usage lies wholly within the framework of the time and cannot be understood adequately if separated from the milieu. Within this milieu slavery was taken for granted. Although Christian emphasis on the value of the person led ultimately to the abolition of the institution, an abolitionist in the first Christian century would have been an anomaly. It is impossible to state apodictically the reason why Paul did not consider the emancipation of the slave to be important. Assuredly, he was interested in social reform. But this was not primary to him. His dominating interest was to preach the gospel. And the Christian gospel brought a freedom which paradoxically was also a slavery.

Paul also delineated another facet of Christian freedom. In contrast to the Greek who was slave to the law, the man in Christ has been freed from this bondage. Here again, Christian freedom from the law is not a human achievement; it is a gift from the divine munificence. Never again need the Christian freedman toil like a slave who endeavors to come to salvation by exact fulfillment of each legal prescription. After Christ takes possession of a man he no longer lives under the rigid domination of the law; for him the

---

[3] Karl H. Rengstorf, "δοῦλος," *Theological Dictionary of the New Testament*, II, 272.

whiplash of external prescription is no more.

Consequently, the Pauline idea of freedom differs radically from that of the Stoics. Despite superficial similarities, it is highly unlikely that the Pauline emphasis on freedom is rooted in stoic thought. The more deeply one penetrates Paul's thinking on liberty, the more evident becomes its profound and intimate Christian nature.

The importance of the Greek translation of the Old Testament as a factor in Paul's hellenistic background should also be recognized. The Septuagint not only prepared the way for the propagation of Christian teachings; it was of paramount importance in the earliest formulation of Christian doctrine. Especially among Jews of the dispersion who studied the Septuagint, Greek terms began very early to take on an hebraic tinge. It is not unreasonable to suppose that Paul, who probably learned the torah in Greek translation or by comparing the Hebrew text with the Septuagint, was to some degree influenced by this aspect of cultural merging. At the very least, it must be acknowledged that by the time Paul proclaimed the gospel to the gentiles, his religious vocabulary had already been created.

A whole gamut of Greek resonances which derived from philosophical reflection upon the life history of Greek cities accompanied Paul's specifically Greek terminology. Upon the base of the Greek ideas of freedom Paul constructed the new and unique Christian concept. Unique though Paul's formulation was, the extent of hellenistic influence upon Paul's synthesis remains to some degree problematic.

Judaic Background

Israel was born of a liberation. From its deliverance from Egyptian bondage Israelite tradition dated its constitution as a nation. Although pagan nations often bound God's people in political servitude, this domination only stimulated the Israelites to think of Yahweh as liberator, he who saves from slavery. Eventually, the prophets defined salvation as the deliverance from a yoke, redemption from oppression, a freedom.

During his Jewish life Paul was proud of belonging to a people chosen by God to receive the messianic liberation. But in the Damascus experience Paul understood that this liberation had been wrought in favor of all sinners who would have faith in Christ. Now Paul realized that grace, not birth, constituted a Christian freedman.

Although the Israelite valued his gift of freedom above all other gifts, in his literature there are few, if any, formal discussions of the subject. Where individual freedom is discussed, it is usually in a legalistic context.[4] Yet the Hebrews revered their God as one who freed his people that they might be in bondage to none but himself. Attributing to Yahweh the institution of the Jubilee, the period during which freedom was granted to all slaves, the Israelites lived in anticipation of the day when his servant would proclaim liberty to the captives (Is 61:1). The conviction of true freedom as being theocentric drove the Qumran extremists into seclusion and the nationalistic Zealots into action. The idea that God is the giver of true liberty is the bedrock of all Paul's teaching on freedom. Greek terms and Christian convictions notwithstanding, the Jewish conviction that freedom is essentially theocentric undergirds the Pauline synthesis of liberty.

The Jewish piety of the first Christian century leaned toward juridicism; the law of God tended to be exalted above God himself. In fact, the rabbis even pretended that Yahweh himself was the first observer of the law which he had promulgated. There were thirty-nine ways of violating the law of the sabbath; consequently, the unlettered man who did not know them was thought incapable of being religious and thereby pleasing to God.

With emphasis on the binding aspects of sabbath observance the pristine significance of the sabbath tended to be

---

[4] See for example Ps 119:44-45.

obscured. Forgotten was the fact that in Egypt the Hebrews were not entitled to rest: the sabbath was the privilege of free men. The note of liberty prominent in the first legislative text on sabbath rest (Ex 23:12) also dominated the deuteronomic reform. The sabbath signified the covenant of salvation, of liberation, and the work customarily performed by slaves (servile work) was not to be performed on this day (Dt 5:12–15). The sabbath, therefore, was originally a visible sign of the liberty granted by God; it was also a sign of man's participation in the divine life. In Paul's day the theology of the sabbath rest hardly influenced the people; strict penalties to compel observance had become necessary. The sabbath was observed because of these penalties, but compliance was, for the most part, superficial and formalistic.

In proclaiming the abrogation of the multiple prescriptions of the law, Paul really brought to fulfillment the pristine notion of law as the privilege of free men. The deep meaning of the sabbath observance, for example, was highlighted in the Pauline declaration of liberation from the slavery of external prescriptions (Gal 4:1–7). Now that God's children had attained maturity, the law had lost its power to enslave. In his maturation the Christian realized the divine liberty of which the sabbath prescriptions were but a feeble sign. In this end time when the Christian community assembled on the first day of the week (1 Cor 16:2), they were to manifest the joy and love that were characteristic of the divine liberty.

It is paradoxical that Paul, who probably did the most to free Christianity from the Jewish law, insisted so vigorously on his upbringing as a Pharisee. By Paul's time Pharisaism was a puritanical movement, completely devoted to the observance of the requirements of the torah; ideally, however, Pharisees were devout and earnest in cultivating the inner life of personal consecration and obedience to the will of God. Not only in his attitude toward the law but also in his allegiance to the great religious affirmations of the early Pharisees, Paul always remained a Pharisee. In the first Christian century Pharisaism was Judaism's most noble expression. Although the effects of the dispersion were not without influence on him, pharisaic Judaism was by far the most formative factor in Paul's background. Both the violence of his initial reaction against the gospel and the cogency with which he later exposed the weakness of life under the law, even while honoring the torah (Rom 7:12), were due in no small part to Paul's training as a Pharisee. Because of his identity as a Pharisee he could attack and defend Judaism from within. Almost every point of Pauline theology was either directly or indirectly developed in response to the Judaizers. Hence the context within which Paul's writings were developed is an important consideration in understanding the total background of his teaching on freedom.

Context of Paul's Teaching on Freedom

Division within the Church is not merely a modern problem; a divisive element was observable in the first Christian century. The Jerusalem Christians practiced circumcision and still adhered to many ritual prescriptions of the torah. Distinguishing between the divine will and Jewish formulations became increasingly difficult for gentile Christians. Gentiles who felt attracted by the Judaizers' point of view acknowledged that Israel had received the promises. The gentiles believed that Israel and Jewish Christianity would be able to attain salvation. However, the dilemma of gentile Christians was both perplexing and disturbing. Apparently, the tension between what is Jewish and what is Christian inheres in Christianity. In the history of the Church the tendency to view the Old Testament in a way not derived from Christ is reminiscent of the Judaizing movement of Paul's time.

Universalism presupposes freedom from legalism. In Paul's day it was not merely a question of the right to preach the gospel to the gentiles; not even the Judaizers questioned this practice. The question was of a more ultimate nature; the very essence of the gospel was questioned. Paul believed that the Christian message was a gospel of unequivocal freedom. Hence he passionately denounced as a betrayal of the gospel and a return to legalistic bondage the adoption by the Galatian Christians of Jewish observances. Realizing that the gospel of freedom and faith was at stake, Paul uncompromisingly took up the challenge of the Judaizers.

In Paul there was an intolerant strain; there is always such a strain in the one who would fight for a new order. Such a man must regard his own convictions as the absolute truth. In this sense, intolerance is essential to progress. Inasmuch as he was intolerant in this sense, Paul could free himself from his past heritage; in his polemic against the Judaizers he gave the pristine Jewish ideal of freedom a fresh religious interpretation.

Galatians 5:1–12 is one of the most forthright statements of Christian freedom. The antithetical drift in the argument comes to expression in an almost ironical way. The freedom which Paul enunciates is liberation from subservience to the law and also from the spiritual impotency from which the law cannot rescue man. Because the salvific thrust of Christ has set man free, falling back into subservience is inexplicable and inexcusable. Paul balances the unequivocal statement: "For freedom Christ has set us free," with the injunction, "Stand fast therefore" (5:1). Although this is an appeal for resolute perseverance in freedom against every effort to bring Christians again under the yoke of slavery, it is not an affirmation of the uselessness of the law. Rather, it is a declaration that outside of Christ the law has no claim upon believers.

Over against the confusion brought about by the Judaizers (5:12), Paul sounded Christ's clear call to freedom (5:13 ff). Affirming that the call to liberty was given with divine sonship, and that this sonship was a gift of the spirit (4:6), Paul exhorted the Galatians to live out this call. To be Christian and to be free, he affirmed, were realities based on the same divine call. Consequently, to separate oneself from this freedom would be to apostasize from grace and from Christ.[5]

"Flesh" (*sárx*) has many connotations in the Pauline epistles. In Gal 5:13, however, the term designates the lower instinct which is always seeking means of self-satisfaction. To hold this tendency in check and to direct the Galatians' daily life, the apostle proposes a norm of conduct which is at the same time a life principle: *agápē*, fruit of the spirit, is also the synthesis of the law. The spirit replaces the precepts of the mosaic law; freedom is the form and expression of the new law. In contradistinction to the yoke[6] of the mosaic law proposed by the Judaizers, Paul enunciates a morality which does not come from external obligation; rather, it is the fruit of inner freedom.

Some misinterpretations of the Pauline synthesis have arisen because modern man tends to lose a sense of the living context in which he wrote. Doctrine separated from life is artificial and misleading. Fluidity of freedom concept, hellenistic influence, judaic background, context: a consideration of these factors leads one to a deeper understanding of the ontological character of Christian freedom.

Inner Character of Christian Freedom

The Spirit, Source of Christian Freedom

Freedom, as Paul viewed it, is not merely a negative concept; it is emancipation from a barren legalism, but it is more. The spirit, creator of a new religious inwardness, is the key to an understanding of the Pauline conception

---

[5] Agapito Güemes, "La ΕΛΕΥΘΕΡΙΑ en las Epistolas Paulinas," *Estudios Biblicos,* 21:1 (Enero-Marzo, 1962), 58.

[6] The yoke was the traditional symbol of slavery. Here the yoke is the mosaic law which keeps man in a state of subservience and fear.

of liberty. Paradoxical as it may seem, when the spirit captivates a man, he is free indeed.

Paul uses *pneûma* mainly to express the power of God's action. Because of the new relationship between God and man, the Christian is said to be in the spirit and to have the spirit in him (Rom 8:9). Giving constant ethical guidance to man, this spirit also gives him a new vitality and radiance (Rom 12:11).

In Romans 5–8 Paul explains the nature of this new free life. Freedom from the wrath of God (Rom 5) leads to liberation from the law (Rom 7). Finally, in Chapter 8, Paul elucidates more fully the freedom of life in the spirit. The longer the relationship with Christ in the spirit continues, the more spontaneously does the Christian produce the fruits of the spirit.

"Now the Lord is the spirit; and where the spirit of the Lord is, there is liberty" (2 Cor 3:17). The meaning of the term "spirit" in this passage is problematic. A consideration of the context, however, leads to an understanding of the term. Here Paul's concern is with the contrast between the old and new covenants; he is not discussing the ontology of trinitarianism. The situation of the Jews, bound to the letter which kills, is contrasted with the situation of Christians who have entered into the liberty of Christ; this dynamic liberty of the spirit is opposed to the mere letter. It is important that the Christian freedman should not return to bondage. Therefore, Paul reminds Christians that the spirit they have received is one of adoption, not of slavery and fear (Rom 8:15).

Although there is no direct reference to the Holy Spirit in this passage (2 Cor 3:17), Paul presupposes the work of the Holy Spirit. Paul consistently taught that the Holy Spirit applies the work of Christ to all men. The action of the spirit effects an essential change in man, a change which has immediate consequences, even in this life. Because of his divine adoption, a new Christian existence, gift of the spirit, is accessible to man. In striving for freedom the Christian works toward the fulfillment of his humanity. The more he realizes his divine sonship, the more human he becomes; simultaneously, his grasp on freedom becomes more secure. Essentially, the divine filiation renders man truly free.

Divine Sonship, Reason for Human Freedom

The power of the spirit progressively delivers man from hereditary servitude; with the attainment of divine sonship man becomes profoundly free. By his birth in bondage under the law Christ enpowered man to live the life of divine sonship, a life of the spirit (Gal 4:4–5).

But the attainment of the divine sonship is a continuing reality. Although the Christian is born in the Spirit and can with assurance call God "Father" (Gal 4:6), complete filiation will be accomplished only in the *éschaton*, in the "end time." In this respect, the Pauline notion is in direct opposition to that of the Greeks. The latter envisioned liberty as basically a good to be attained in the present life. Christian freedom is an ever new gift of the Holy Spirit. It never freezes nor coagulates into a purely human possession because it is a life, not a thing.[7]

In the Pauline synthesis the theme of Christian liberty is intimately connected with the allegory of Sara and Agar (Gal 4:22–31). Agar, the slave girl, represents the Jewish nation enslaved by the law. Sara, the free woman, represents the heavenly Jerusalem; she gives birth to the heir of the promised filiation. The nature of the freedom enjoyed by the sons of God becomes clearer by the contrast with the opposite, the condition of slavery. Slaves and heirs may perform identical acts; however, the spirit that animates

---

[7] Jean Mouroux, *The Christian Experience*, trans. George Lamb (New York: Sheed and Ward, 1954), p. 138, nicely expresses the continuing nature of Christian freedom when he writes: "Man is liberated completely but imperfectly — first, because though he is liberated in spirit he is not liberated in body except in hope . . . , and secondly because even his spirit is only liberated as something to which victory has been promised, not given, so that it has to be fought for."

them differs radically. The former obey in fear; the latter obey in love. A filial morality is one based on love. Having initiated man into a state of sonship, the Holy Spirit teaches him to think, act, and love as a son. Progressively, the spirit creates in the sons of God a Christian mentality. Basically, this is a mentality of divine liberty. In the power of the spirit man partakes in the freedom of the Son, who being fully divine, is at the same time intensely human and free.

In Rom 8:14–16 Paul affirms that Christian freedom is a sharing in the freedom of the Son before the Father. The spirit interiorly urges man toward an ever fuller share in this freedom. This filial freedom rises from the very center of man's being; in the confrontation with total reality man's whole being expresses itself in an ever-increasing Christian freedom. Spirit, freedom, divine filiation: each one of these concepts implies and enriches the others.

The Indicative, Ground of the Imperative

Repeatedly, Paul assumes a radical change in Christians. Quite certainly, the imperative is rooted in the indicative (Gal 5:24 ff). In obeying, in walking according to the spirit, the Christian becomes what he already is. The command to walk by the spirit (Gal 5:16 ff) concludes with the paradoxical injunction: "If we live by the spirit, let us also walk by the spirit" (Gal 5:25). The purpose of this formulation is to avoid the misunderstanding that a walking by the spirit would be necessary to establish a living by the spirit. Upon reflection Paul's meaning becomes clear: the indicative is foundation for the imperative.

In the New Testament proclamation many statements in the indicative mood assume that the new creation is an accomplished fact. Other statements, however, seem to indicate that Christian existence is not yet a complete reality; its actualization demands human decision. This double dimension in the Christian proclamation shows that indicative and imperative cannot be separated; rather, they belong together as two sides of a coin. Christian obedience means to obey the imperative that is embodied in the indicative.[8]

Obedience to God is freedom. The liberty to obey is the freedom for which man was set free by the salvation occurrence. The liberty which Paul preached is properly understood neither as a release from binding norms nor from the law of God. It is an enslavement to righteousness; it is obedience to God rather than obedience to *sárx*. Freedom is realized in obedience, and obedience is accomplished in freedom. Both a striving to be what one already is and an obedience which is never an accomplished fact: this is the tension of Christian existence.

The marvel of the Christian indicative lies in its intimate union with the imperative. In the Christian, indicative and imperative become one. Because he is a new creature, the Christian obeys his divine Father. Obeying, he is truly free, but his freedom does not derive from his human action. Rather, the spirit of Christ which inheres in him makes possible this free Christian existence. The very essence of the Son, the state of existing completely in and for the Father, presupposes communion with the Father in the spirit. In his Christian relationships regenerated man is called to reflect the freedom in unity of the Trinity.

Communal Implications of Christian Freedom

Emphasis on Community

At his conversion Paul underwent an experience that was intensely personal; yet it involved the Christian community. The realization that Christ was present in his members deepened progressively after he became a member of the Christian community. However deeply personal the experience of the spirit, it relates to the Church.

Perhaps Paul's conception of human freedom differs most

---

[8] Thomas Oden, *Radical Obedience* (Philadelphia: The Westminster Press, 1964), pp. 94–95.

strikingly from the hellenistic notion in its emphasis on the communal character of Christian freedom. Under the guidance of the spirit the Christian community finds freedom in a truly cooperative way. The unity of all men is a presupposition transferred without challenge from Judaism and the Old Testament into Paul's writings. Paul's Jewish monotheism is the threshold of his doctrine on the unity of all mankind. But his dual emphasis upon the individual as under the guidance of the spirit and on a community composed of spirit-guided individuals is original.

The frequency with which Paul had to battle against antinomianism indicates the enthusiasm with which the message of liberation was received. In clarifying misunderstanding of the true nature of Christian freedom, Paul showed that the Church was not made up of individuals placed side by side, each seeking his own autonomy; rather, he affirmed that the Christian, a member of a community, lives his life in the context of other people. To identify freedom with autonomy means to exchange Christian liberty for slavery to sin and lawlessness. In this life Christian freedom requires a struggle against the revolt of a selfish nature and an ability to detect the camouflages of false liberty.

Although not all differences within the Christian community can be eliminated, divisions should not exist. Christ has shown his followers how to welcome freely the other in his otherness. He welcomed sinners; he welcomed even those who resisted him. To welcome one another in all diversity, even in opposition: this is the essence of love, a love which guarantees the unity of the Christian community. In the present time tension exists on all levels within the Christian community. The free welcoming of one another in diversity will make this tension fruitful. This welcoming of one another is love, and in the Christian dispensation love is supreme.

Because Paul conceived of agápē as providing the controlling force for the moral conduct of Christians, he set it sharply against the law and trusted those moved by love to fulfill the law freely. Every neophyte experienced this liberation, but some of them did not understand the exclusively spiritual nature of their new liberty. In Corinth some thought that Christian freedom meant that slaves were automatically freed from their masters. And more Corinthians prided themselves on the freedom their knowledge gave them. Instead of correcting their erroneous ideas directly, Paul gave them a higher principle. He affirmed that love was a form of slavery (1 Cor 9:19), binding the Christian to his brother (Gal 5:13). Thus the gnostic mentality and Christian mentality were clearly distinguished.

Paul vigorously defended the moral autonomy of the Christian; however, his emphasis upon moral autonomy was balanced by his delineation of the nature of the body of Christ. In this body the spirit is a corporate, as well as an individual, possession, and the community which is nourished by the *agápē* of God in Christ is a safe guide to the requirements of love in the life of the people of God. Insofar as she lives out the demands of this love, the Church guarantees to her sons the freedom which is their heritage.

Love, Inner Conditioner of Liberty

The man who loves is most completely free. The law of the spirit enjoins everything contained in the human law with requirements much more exacting; it is the compelling urge of a son's love to do everything possible to please the Father. Paul's conception of the perfect Christian is a son, filled with the spirit, in love with God and with his brethren. The only limitation that Paul put upon freedom was that imposed by love. In his mutual relationships man is called to reflect the love life of the triune God. The power of this love limits the irrational and destructive possibilities of man's quest for pure freedom; this limitation transforms pure freedom into responsible freedom.

The Christian freedman, member of the new covenant

community, is bound no longer by the external law of works; rather, his freedom is regulated by the inward law of love. Christ's love draws man in and relates him to his brothers in loving fellowship. From man's personal freedom grows his corporate freedom which is expressed in the Christian community. Whenever man separates himself from his brothers, he mutilates his freedom. Whence the dialectical relation, eventually the dialectical tension, between person and community.

Love's struggle begins and ends within man. He is made for a love relationship, but involvement with his brother threatens his selfishness. Therefore, ruse enables him to avoid the dialogue which is love. Hate is quite straightforward; love is ambiguous, a selfish urge to devour the other frequently masquerades as love. That is why Paul proceeded so carefully when he wrote of the power of God's love (Rom 12:9–21). It is no accident that the first thing he wrote about it was that it must not be false (v. 9). Existential love is dangerous, but it is the Christian imperative. Either man finds God in his brother, or he finds him not at all. In his death-thrust for communion Christ perfectly realized his human freedom.

Basically, the morality which Paul preached is one of love and therefore of freedom. But compulsory love is no love at all. Led by the spirit and acting in virtue of this inner principle, the Christian is free, released from outside pressure; yet he is not a victim of his own whims. Paul regards love more as conditioning the Christian's freedom than as directing it. As the will of God is central in the guidance of liberty, so the love of God (both his love for man and man's response) is central in this conditioning. The necessity of love within the Christian community was so basic to Paul's thought and teaching that he could write to the Thessalonians: "But concerning love of the brethren you have no need to have anyone write to you, for you yourselves have been taught by God to love one another" (1 Th 4:9).

The way in which the apostle demonstrated his love is one of the best illustrations of the nature of this inward conditioner of Christian freedom.

Law, External Regulator of Freedom

A remarkable and puzzling feature of Paul's experience was that he found that only law could liberate from law. When he became a Christian, Paul did not cast off restraint; he submitted to a new law. But the context of Rom 8:2 shows law not so much a set of rules as a regulative principle. Law and freedom are not diametrically opposed. Rather, the law of the spirit brings freedom. Given wherever communion with Christ in his brothers really exists, the spirit brings life. Freedom is found in communion; elsewhere man is in his own imprisonment.

In the sense that it implies a searching criticism of mere outward conformity to moral claims, the spirit of Paul's ethics is antilegalistic. Although Paul outlawed superficial legality, his synthesis was not anti-legal. What the spirit wrote on the hearts of men remained the law. In the time of the spirit the commandments were not to be rejected; they were to be fulfilled in the most profound sense. The Christian is not a lawless rebel. Grace shapes him into an ever more perfect image of the changeless Lawgiver. Particularly in Christ man knows that he is subject to the law, that is, to the demand for complete truth, purity, and love; this is God's will. But man's highest goodness is never his achievement in obedience to the law; this is God's gracious gift. The gift of the spirit constitutes the Christian (Rom 8:9).

In an individual Christian, full liberty characterizes spiritual maturity. According to Paul, the perfect are those who have fully delivered themselves to the spirit. Only these are completely free. On the contrary, a preponderance of precepts characterizes the life of beginners (Gal 4:3). As an individual reaches Christian maturity, he attains freedom, at first restricted, then total. The disengagement from external constraints is a constant struggle in the present life.

Although Paul was saddened when he found envy, strife, jealousy, and factions in the Christian community, he did not attribute these disorders to the inadequacy of the new life; rather, he acknowledged that these ills were symptoms of immaturity. Paul did not surrender his belief in the Christian's essential freedom from external constraints; however, at times he found it necessary to appeal to the more tangible standards of personal example to regulate the Christian life in his congregations. True, he used external standards and examples to direct the lives of immature Christians; however, he used these standards and examples sparingly. He intended them only as temporary inducements to guide Christians in their attainment of complete Christian freedom.

Paschal Nature of Christian Freedom

Christ's Work of Freedom

Christ's work of paschal freedom dominated Paul's thought. Because his life was wholly conformed to the will of his Father, Christ was free before the law. Above all, he was free from death. Although he suffered physical death, Christ did not undergo what the scriptures mean by death: the confirmation of final separation from God. In fact, Christ's physical death was the way to true life, the door of joyous return to the Father.

Christ's earthly mission, the freeing of his fellow men from the burden of their own selfishness, was but the beginning of the liberating mission that burst upon the world with saving energy at the moment of the resurrection. When earthly bonds were broken, the power of the Father became all Christ's to use; the spirit of the Father, all his to give.

In his paschal action Christ has left slavery forever. The spirit, God's spontaneity breaking out into the world, knows no coercion. Henceforth, all limitations inherent in Christ's human nature are gone; gone is the need to be subject to any law other than the law of the spirit, the law which belongs to his new life. The work of the spirit eventuates in Christ's unfettered liberty, his entry into his inheritance, and his exaltation in power.

In the life of the early Church there was an increasing awareness of the liberating effect of Christ's whole work. However, someone was needed to delineate the new life of freedom in terms of lasting principles. That someone was Paul. He expressed the drama of Christ's liberating work in symbolic language. The most consistent note in the Pauline synthesis of redemption is that of participation. Paul expressed man's sin and need in terms of participation in Adam and his sin. Christ came into the world to participate in human life; his death and man's baptism effect man's participation in the death action that liberates. When Paul wrote of man's participation in the resurrection and ascension, the symbolism was obscure. Man has truly risen with Christ and shares in the freedom that resurrection brings, but his mortal body has not been entirely freed and will not be until Christ returns in glory. Thus the tension between the already and the not yet is evident also in man's participation in the liberating paschal action. The dialectic of slavery and freedom is transposed into a dialectic of death and life, of death to the present world, of anticipated entrance into the free world of the resurrection.

Christ's death, which showed his filial obedience and manifested the Father's love for men, and his resurrection, which revealed his constitution as Son of God in power, was a secure pledge of man's ultimate total freedom. One day, through the indwelling Spirit, the Father who freed Jesus from the bonds of death will certainly give man the fullness of salvation, the freedom of resurrection life.[9] In the present,

---

[9] David Michael Stanley, *Christ's Resurrection in Pauline Soteriology* (Romae, e Pontificio Instituto Biblico, 1961), p. 286.

however, the baptismal action of Christ is at once pledge and inauguration of the Christian into the liberty of the resurrected.

Baptismal Sharing in Christ's Liberating Action

In the old covenant the people of God were baptized into Moses. In the new dispensation God's people are baptized into Christ; they are brought from death to life, from slavery to freedom. In both instances the oneness of the people thus formed rests on a common deliverance, a great act of divine mercy. However, there is a fundamental difference. The relationship effected by the baptism of Moses materialized in obedience to the law; the relationship effected by Christian baptism gives believers a share in Christ's freedom from the law.

Materially and in time, the love of God, enacted once for all in Christ's death and resurrection, is accomplished in Christian baptism. Likewise, the incursion of the spirit in the liberating paschal event frees man in sacramental action. Because of the baptismal act in which the spirit of Christ's love is given to man, the Christian is bound to acknowledge the claim of liberating love. The incursion of God's love has released man from the bondage of sin; in view of this invasion man must continually decide for the love which presses in upon him. Essentially, the gospel is a call to respond to the paschal act of Jesus Christ as the basis of a new life of freedom.

In baptism the Christian becomes a new creature. This newness of being demands a new life. No longer a slave of the law, the Christian freedman is committed to acting on a plane commensurate with his new state. Existentially, some Christians are not yet convinced that they are really free in Christ. Submitting to the demands of Christian morality as to a heavy burden imposed from without, they conform with the demeanor of a slave. Only when he takes his resurrection seriously will the follower of Christ find peace, joy, and freedom. Then he will see the demands of the Christian life as the deepest expression of his interior being rather than as restraints or taboos.

Baptism is also an act of appropriation by which Christ obtains the ownership of a man, and the latter becomes Christ's slave. In the paschal action Christ has, in a sense, gained possession of the Christian. When Paul presents this idea he links it precisely to the statement that believers are free from the mastery of all else because they have become slaves of Christ. This statement gives rise to Paul's dialectic of the liberty and bondage of the baptized.

To understand Paul's dialectic, it is important to remember that in biblical times servants were usually slaves, the property of their masters. So 'ebed sometimes means "slave." However, in ancient Israel the condition of a slave was neither ignominious nor irksome; the bondage of the individual slave was quite different from the forced servitude of a whole people, as, for example, that of the Hebrews in Egypt.

The nearest Greek equivalent for the Hebrew 'ebed was doûlos, which in its strict sense referred to one born in slavery. So in ordinary Greek it could hardly be used of a servant who was not a slave. Paul often called Christians the servants (doûloi) of Christ, the primary significance being that Christians, having been bought with a price (1 Cor 6:20; 7:23), belonged to their master. But Paul also insisted that Christ freed men from every other kind of bondage. Now Christians are no longer slaves; they are sons of God. In the Pauline epistles the precise meaning of the noun doûlos and the corresponding verb varies according to the context. For example, in 1 Cor 7:23 Paul enjoins Christians not to become slaves of men; in Col 3:22 he bids those who are slaves in the literal sense to obey their earthly masters, and in Gal 5:13 Paul enjoins Christians to serve (be slaves to) one another in love.

Assuredly, in this world the Christian will experience conflicts, since the flesh still wars against the spirit. The tension between the slavery which brings death and that which brings

the life of Christian freedom is very real in this time in between. However, a Christian personality is not formed from
the elimination of conflict; rather, it is formed from an inte-
gration of all its inclinations into the synthesis of the new life
of the resurrection.

Realization of the Freedom of
Life in the Spirit

Freedom from sin and the law culminates in freedom from
death. Human works done in freedom produce that which
underlies them, namely, the eternity disclosed in the event of
Christ's love. These works express Christian freedom which
makes possible for the neighbor the life which one himself
enjoys. True, freedom from death is enacted only within an
existence which is still given up to death. But man knows
freedom from death in the resurrection of Jesus Christ which
has been made present by the action of the sacrament. The
works of freedom manifest eternity as that which is still to
come to man in Jesus Christ. When the children of God shine
forth in glory, this liberation will be consummated.

This final freedom will be not merely a liberation from the
tyranny of sin, the law, and death; it will be also a participation in the divine glory. Having fulfilled his destiny within
the framework of the new creation, the new creature will
possess a liberty wherein the glory of the creator is fully manifested. The fundamental renewal of man's being will be
matched by a renewal of the life of the world, for the ultimate hope of faith must be extended to the creative process
as a whole.

Paul's most profound and characteristic expression of the
theology of baptism, that of dying and rising with Christ, also
emphasizes man's liberation which is its consequence. Baptism speaks of man's oneness with Christ, his witness to Christ,
his new freedom, and his new bondage. Freed from the bonds
of sin and death, man is bound no less certainly to the divine

will and incorporated into the fellowship of all who are in Christ. The Christian does not have to choose between a liberty which is license and some other legalism which is just as compelling as the old. His way of liberty is love, a love which works itself out with others and for others. Expressing itself in a willingness to share the burdens of others, in a freedom to serve, in an ordering of itself to the needs of the corporate life, this love is both the pre-condition and the result of a liberty which is not to degenerate into license or surrender to legalism.

"For you were called to freedom, brethren; only do not use your freedom as an opportunity for the flesh, but through love be servants [slaves] of one another" (Gal 5:13). With this statement Paul resolves the supposed opposition between freedom and the Christian law. Christian freedom is- the most demanding of callings — a call to love — and nothing is more demanding than love. Indeed, the apostle uses the strongest expression possible; he exhorts the Galatians to be *slaves* to one another. Christian life, therefore, is slavery. But it is a slavery of love and, therefore, supreme freedom.

Fundamentally, Christian freedom is liberation from the slavery of sin, the law, and death. This liberation, realized by Christ, is given to man by faith and baptism. Christian liberty is the possibility of attaching man again to God; it is a freedom of sonship. It is a freedom of service which works for the building up of the Christian community. At the parousia, the time of maturity, the Christian will finally attain to perfect freedom which Paul called "the glorious liberty of the children of God" (Rom 8:21).

CHAPTER IV

CONTEMPORARY MORAL CATECHESIS

Dilemma of Modern Moral Catechesis

In the contemporary outlook on morals confusion appears more common than clarification. The moral life of many modern men is characterized by irresolution. On the one hand, they cling to certain directives of traditional morality, while on the other they experiment with new forms in an effort to live a satisfying life in the modern world. The result is a moral alienation which is an integral part of the more generic problem of alienation that is characteristic of modern times.

The widespread belief that the old morality is no longer adapted to twentieth-century living has seriously compromised the universal character of morality. In an attempt to remedy the moral crisis, some eminent thinkers have identified morality with mores; moral rectitude is measured in terms of conformity with the most generalized practice in a given social group. Although within closed societies that were ignorant of other social groups morality was identified with mores, from his privileged position of posteriority modern man can easily discern the inadequacy of such a morality.

A morality based solely on mores would not merit the name of morality. By definition morality is normative; its purpose is not to conserve a system of mores. Rather, the development of a system of mores which is consonant with the realization of human potentialities is not the least among the functions of a Christian morality.

Certainly, as a believer the Christian is no longer under the law; however, as a sinner he finds himself subject to it. Perhaps this uncomfortable dialectic of gospel and law has been more consciously experienced by Protestants than by Catholics. Critics of bad catechetical practice charge that the latter have been indoctrinated in a caricature of Christian life dominated by a multiplicity of precepts and prohibitions worked out into the minutest detail with hairsplitting rabbinism.[1] Both groups, however, have tended to develop a legalism which has confronted man with an impossible ethic and brought him into constant conflict with God and with himself.

Caught in a legalistic vise, some men try to free themselves by using the device of an ethics of situation. In extracting himself from the bind of legalism, an individual may take any one of a wide range of positions which hold an ethics of situation. At one extreme, he may acknowledge as norm of action only the call of each unique situation which he must respond to successfully. In doing so, he may deny the validity of any objective norm which can bind in the concrete situation. This solution conceives the human person as an individual who is absolutely and in every respect unique.[2] On the other hand, an individual may regard a situation as giving the clue for the choice of universal norms applicable here and now. The difficulty in discovering the moral imperative in the concrete is seen to lie only in the exactness and adequacy of the analysis of the concrete situation.

Although on the surface the latter may appear to be a simple solution to the modern moral dilemma, the ambiguity

---

[1] Louis Monden, *Sin, Liberty and Law*, trans. Joseph Donceel (New York: Sheed and Ward, Inc., 1965), p. 84.

[2] Karl Rahner, "On the Question of a Formal Existential Ethics," *Theological Investigations*, Vol. II: *Man in the Church*, trans. Karl-H. Kruger (Baltimore: Helicon Press, 1963), 218–219.

of the situation and the difficulty in making a clear-cut application of universal norms negates the simplistic character of any proposed answer. While acknowledging the inadequacy of the existentialist solution, many regard existentialism as a valuable protest against various contemporary forms of impersonalism. Certainly, today's moral dilemma cries out for a reconstruction of the Christian ethic.

By this revolt against a rigid application of universal norms the existentialist tries to make an ethical adjustment to the modern situation. Although it may be true that in so doing he has proposed a nineteenth-century answer to a twentieth-century dilemma,[3] the need for a determination of morality in view of the existential situation has induced many men to grasp at this solution. The basic immaturity of the existentialist answer which unknowingly seeks an ultimate explanation of reality has prevented the giving of a satisfying answer to a basic question: has modern man no norm against which he may measure his conduct? Abandonment solely to his own experience is likely to drive a man to despair.

The double standard which acknowledged the tension between the ideal and the actual no longer provides the comfortable security that it did yesteryear. Now the catechist has found that he must take the risk of speaking to actual ethical situations lest his message evaporate into vapid moralizing. Man lives his life in a particular place, doing a certain job, faced with specific issues; generic and abstract ethical pronouncements do not interest him. Today's catechist finds himself in a dilemma that is not unrelated to the quandary in which Paul found himself in another aeon. The real continuities of the contemporary moral situation with that of

---

[3] Harvey Cox, *The Secular City* (New York: The Macmillan Company, 1965), p. 252. The exact basis for this charge is problematic. However, the context indicates that Cox believes that existentialists revolt against a metaphysical tradition which died with the nineteenth century. Speaking in metaphysical categories of yesterday (Cox acknowledges that existentialists would deny this), the existentialists fail to communicate with the secular-urban world of today.

Paul's day seem to be submerged beneath apparent discontinuities. The catechist must strain to understand and apply the very real continuous element in the law to modern living. Two emphases reflected in contemporary thinking and writing have influenced the climate within which the moral synthesis must be constructed. Emphasis on the solidarity of sacred and profane has, in a certain sense, been complementary to the contrasting of open and closed moralities. A discussion of these two facets of modern thought may help to delineate more clearly the modern catechetical dilemma.

Solidarity of Sacred and Profane

Tension between the sacred and the profane has been experienced in varying degrees in the history of mankind. From a magical identification of the two spheres, man passed to an ontological way of thinking in which he separated the sacred from the profane. Though separate, the two spheres were still in some way connected. In the medieval university, for example, the natural and the supernatural were thought of in much the same manner as different floors in the same building.

In the modern secularized world a functional way of thinking appears to have superseded the former ontological view. In this era reality seems to be that which functions; only that which directly relates to mundane living seems real. On the surface such an outlook may seem to negate the sacred. Dietrich Bonhoeffer's insistence on finding a nonreligious interpretation of the gospel for modern man apparently reinforces this view. However, Bonhoeffer also affirmed that in its coming of age the world is more godless, and perhaps for that very reason nearer to God than ever before.[4] Modern man's disregard for the sacred is perhaps but a cloak which hides a deep unity of the sacred with the secular. Indeed, it can happen that the most radical expression of

---

[4] Dietrich Bonhoeffer, Prisoner for God, ed. Eberhard Bethge, trans. Reginald Fuller (New York: The Macmillan Company, 1959), p. 167.

profane existence coincides with the highest expression of the sacred.

In Christ the radical separation between sacred and profane has not simply been transcended; it has been broken down. In the act of restoring man to a full grace-relationship with his creator Christ is the unification of God and man (i.e., the epitome of a *cosmos* alienated from God). Not that there is an identification between them. But in Christ the human race, all human activity, and all creation are assumed into a new relationship with God. After the incarnation nothing is the same; a sacred relationship enters into all of man's living.

No longer can the Christian regard his earthly existence merely as a prologue to his future life in a transcendent kingdom. Neither can he hold that his secular life gets its meaning and reality only from another life in the realm of the sacred. The discovery that the Spirit is at work recreating the secular from within has made possible a new epiphany of Christ. Not a substitute for an absent Christ, the Holy Spirit is the agent of Christ's presence in the world. Thus Christendom has given birth to a radically profane consciousness, and this secular existence has proved to be the way to a Christ who is fully incarnate in the midst of the world.[5]

Whether he knows it or not, modern man is alienated neither from the secular nor from the sacred. The sacred interpenetrates the secular; through the secular the sacred is revealed. The sight of a newborn child, contact with an object of devotion, the encounter with a person who is somehow different, can bring a profound realization of the sacred into an atmosphere that was thought to be completely secular.

In witnessing to the solidarity of sacred and secular, these instances also manifest the mysterious nature of the

[5] Thomas J. J. Altizer, *Mircea Eliade and the Dialectic of the Sacred* (Philadelphia: The Westminster Press, 1963), p. 18.

unity. One is led to a deeper comprehension of the meaning of Teilhard de Chardin's statement that in the practical sphere true union does not confound; it differentiates.[6] Sometimes most unexpectedly modern man echoes the sentiments of Jacob: "Surely the Lord is in this place; and I did not know it" (Gen 28:16).

Secular and sacred, historical and eschatological, natural and supernatural — these dualities indicate the same primary truths. On the one hand, man's life must be lived out in the world of space and time. On the other hand, the ultimate foundation of this life lies in a supratemporal relation to the reality which transcends creaturely existence. Minimizing either aspect of this two-sidedness of human life risks stripping life of meaning.

The Christian task is to express objectively the God-related life in its secularity. If the catechist can give his students the courage to be truly secular, he will not have to worry about the relevance of their witness. Their testimony to the solidarity of sacred and secular will itself be a lifegiving incarnation. Their worldliness will not separate them from Christ; their Christianity will not divide them from the world. Belonging wholly to Christ, they will stand at the same time wholly in the world.

Open and Closed Moralities

From the time that intelligent beings begin to come in contact with one another they have felt the need to guard themselves against their mutual encroachments. Principally, a fixed system of rights and duties, this primitive morality sought to establish a static equilibrium among individuals; reduction of friction was a prime consideration. This conception of morality rests on the belief that each person represents a sort of absolute end; he must protect his existence against all exterior invasion.

---

[6] Pierre Teilhard de Chardin, *The Future of Man*, trans. Norman Denny (New York: Harper and Row, Publishers, 1964), p. 53.

In distinguishing between the foregoing moral system which he terms an open morality, Bergson characterizes the first as social and the second as human. The first morality is comparatively easy to formulate; it is immutable, static, and gives a certain sense of security. But this security is the security of death. Movement is one certain sign of life; adherence to immutable laws effectively imprisons man in the group. This is a code morality, one which ensures the cohesion of the group by bending all wills to the same end. In this system law exerts pressure to maintain the static equilibrium of the group.

Much more difficult to formulate is the second, radically different type of morality. An open morality is one of movement; it is human instead of being merely social. Modern man has experienced an increasing tension between established norms and the new norms which his situation in history seems to impose. He has demanded a morality which recognizes his right to behave as a person, which he freely accepts as a person, and which suits his historical situation. Inadvertently, perhaps, modern man has realized that to be a Christian does not consist in the following of some rigid moral code; neither does it demand the cultivation of some particular form of asceticism. To be a Christian is, at the very least, to be a man. There is, of course, a radical distinction between nature and grace, but there is also an intimate connection between them. Caught up by Christ's consecration of the universe to his heavenly Father, the world of nature has begun the growth which will come to fruition when the universe (the world of nature and the world of grace) is handed over by Christ to the Father.

Three principles enumerated by Teilhard de Chardin are both indicative of the spirit of the new morality and evaluative of the character of human acts. (1) Nothing is finally good except that which helps to build the spirit on the earth; (2) everything is at least partially good which helps toward the spiritual growth of the earth; (3) that is morally best which assures the highest development of the spiritual elements of the earth.[7] Deep understanding of the Pauline emphasis on the work of the spirit in the world would seem to be necessary for a comprehension of Teilhard's meaning. Teilhard's cosmic view of Christ demands a revamping of Christian moral ethics. Likewise, an open morality, a living out of the life in Christ in the world, was the timeless Pauline exhortation. Creative surrender to the guidance of the spirit will lead to full Christian and human realization.

But progress from a closed to an open morality is not inevitable; the tendency to slip back into a fixed code morality seems to be inherent in man's temporal existence. The less a man knows of the true meaning of God's love, the more likely he is to need the guidance of external law. In his present condition of limited awareness of the meaning of God's love the Christian requires some external moral direction. While recognizing that some code morality is relatively inevitable, the Christian catechist should try to lead his students from a static group morality to an authentic morality of the human person. Concretely, he will stimulate them to overcome their selfishness sufficiently to live for others. Christ has revealed the possibility of doing this. The anonymous ideal of everyman has been given a name in Jesus Christ; with that name came the guarantee that the ideal could be approached. Certainly, in taking to heart the great concerns of this world, the Christian acts in a manner that is consonant with the divine love which is his life.

The distinction between closed and open moralities is analogous to the Pauline distinction between letter and spirit. The letter kills not merely because it judges him who cannot fulfill the law; it is deadening in its suppression of the creative potentialities of the unique moment which never was before and which never will come again. On the contrary, in determining the decisions of life in a particular situation,

---

[7] Pierre Teilhard de Chardin, L'Énergie Humaine (Paris: Éditions du Seuil, 1962), pp. 132–133.

the spirit opens the individual to the potentialities of the moment. Thus the problem of the absolute and relative character of the moral imperative is solved in principle. As the ultimate principle of morality love is always the same; entering the unique situation in the power of the spirit, love is always different.

Ideally, the Christian is guided by the spirit. Thus, in the Pauline synthesis the law of Christ (Gal 6:2; 1 Cor 9:12) excels the mosaic law, not as a higher moral code excels a more primitive one, but as the lifegiving spirit excels the death-bringing letter (2 Cor 3:6; Rom 7:6). Because the majority of Christians are sinners, however, the ideal is rarely attained. Normally a practical necessity, external rules of Christian conduct always remain secondary to the law of the spirit. Moreover, they have a *raison d'être* only insofar as they are somehow the expression of Christ's love.

Rigid adherence to the letter of the law brings a tyranny which is as static and deadening as it is impersonal. A Christian open morality, concerned as much with the integrity of the individual as with the good of the group, is both sensitive to the exigencies of concrete situations and aware of the needs of the community. The fullest possible realization of a responsible and effective love is the aim of an open morality.

Nature of Christian Morality

The nature of Christian morality is problematic; basic ambiguities revolve around the proper place of the law in Christian existence. The contemporary crisis in morality is the deepest expression of the long-standing tension between law and spirit. One of the most vexing problems faced by the modern catechist is precisely that of the proper situating of legal codes in the Christian life.

A general agreement that Christian morality concerns the behavior of men called to be new creatures merely gives the basis for a debate which has been often heated, always lively. The search for perfection as the primary principle of morality has issued in exaggerated emphasis on the law and the works of the law as tangible assurance of this perfection. Perfectionism, or hypermorality, is just as dangerous to moral health as the other extreme of refusing to recognize any moral obligation. The task of morality is to produce men who realize their vocation in the community of men. It is not to stimulate men to herculean feats of moral and physical endurance. True Christian morality is a relationship with God and man that is positive and is experienced in the ever-deepening search for communion. It is neither a morality of duty nor of acts; essentially, it is an ethic of love.

Emphasis on juridical aspects has resulted in a decreased emphasis on morality as a way of living and acting proportioned to the new life in Christ. In the Christian perspective the behavior of man is a personal and free response to the divine call. Christian morality is the deliberate and considered orientation of this behavior. Since it was made to guide this deliberate orientation, the moral law is in a number of important aspects relative. It is both the means of acknowledging man's fall from grace and the framework within which he seeks to respond to the love of God.

Too often Christianity is confused with simple morality; the very rhythm of the religious life, the frequentation of the sacraments, is presented exclusively as an obligatory rule of procedure. A way of presenting the positive instructions of the Church that concentrates on minutiae, as for example the amount of work permitted on Sundays, ends by gravely falsifying religious education. How often young people think they reject religion when what they really are doing is reacting against the caricature that has been presented as the essence of religion. Legalism engenders lawlessness;

nomism leads to antinomism; perfectionism may terminate in libertinism.

Either the Christian must point to something that transcends both graceless moralism and normless relativism or he will be completely divorced from a secular existence which is at the same time implicitly Christian. Christianity's response that a new reality, a power of being from which right action can follow, has appeared with the coming of Christ, stands in opposition to both moral legalism and amoral lawlessness.

The Christian life begins and ends with God. Ultimately, it is a God-centered life rather than a self-centered life. Christian moral living begins with God's gift of grace in Christ, the means of discovering the deepest meaning of love possible in human life. It ends with God's grace nurturing a growing relationship of love for him and others, a relationship which leads to the highest creative affirmation of the human personality.

Sin, Negation of Christian Moral Relationship

Even when man knows that the purpose of life is realized in relationship with God, he often rebels and tries to walk alone. No single factor in human living is more destructive than sin because sin estranges man from the ground of his being. Alienating himself from the One for whom he longs, man finds his life distorted, frustrated, and broken. Attempting to live with the gods of his own making rather than with the uncreated One, man often turns away from God, donor of freedom and ability to respond.

Thus, sin is not a thing. It is a refusal to respond to love; it is an absence of life; it is sickness and shame. Catechesis on sin should always be given within the context of the Christian mystery. Catechesis on God, our sovereign and holy Father; on Christ in his paschal gesture, and on the Holy Spirit who expresses the divine love in the union of men with their brothers, lays the ground for imparting an authentic sense of sin.[8]

A world which has denied the existence of sin inarticulately strives for relief from the guilt feelings which oppress it. In a moral system which denies sin man is responsible only before others; in a morality which recognizes sin, man is also responsible before God. By conveying an authentic sense of sin, moral catechesis simultaneously develops moral response-ability. Neither a juridical concept nor a neurotic projection of unconscious taboos, sin signifies the reference of human acts to an absolute, to God. The idea of sin is not identical with a morality founded upon fear; a spirituality and a morality inspired by natural generosity and supernatural charity also encompasses the sense of sin as a basic premise.

An authentic catechesis on sin contrasts a life of Christian responsibility and one of sinful irresponsibility. If Christians were to understand sin as a rejection of responsibility, as a destruction of the ability to respond to divine love, they would, perhaps, be better able to achieve a satisfactory synthesis of gospel and law. Daily sharing in the divine responsibility would render Christians ever more capable of responding in love to an infinitely loving Father. Then the paralysis of sin would disappear. And fear would no longer dominate man's moral acts.

Identification of Christian Morality

Contemporary discussion as to the nature of Christian morality has been subsumed in a debate between roughly delineated parties representing, on the one hand, allegiance to the use of formal prescriptive principles and, on the other hand, those representing the cause of a more existential response to a particular situation. This debate has forced an unfair polarization upon a diversity of opinions that makes

[8] François Coudreau, "Catechesis and Sin," *Sin*, trans. Bernard Murchland and Raymond Meyerpeter (New York: The Macmillan Company, 1962), pp. 73–77, gives specific indications for adapting the catechesis on sin to Christians of various ages.

it both academically unjust and morally fruitless. The fact that contextualists find some moral principles which guide existential decisions and that the defenders of principles find ways to proceed from generalizations to particular situations has frequently been ignored.[9]

This debate has also tended to obscure the nature of the distinctively Christian moral decision. To hold that such a moral decision is always addressed to a particular situation and never adequately definable simply in terms of the principle behind it is not equivalent to holding that Christian morals are completely relative. Christian moral behavior cannot be separated from its relationship with the immutable God who revealed himself in Jesus Christ. The absolute element in each moral decision is its relationship to God incarnated in Christ; the relative aspect is the application of timeless imperatives to the given situation. The mosaic code forms part, but only part, of the moral background for Christian moral decisions. In Christian moral living there is room neither for the complete rejection of mosaic formulations nor for the acceptance of any system af casuistry evolved from Moses by legalists.[10] Those who equate Christianity with a fixed code of conduct, valid for all Christians at all times, err by identifying religion and morality.

It is important to distinguish between religion and morality; however, such a distinction in no way implies a radical separation between the two. Identifying a given morality with the Christian religion has resulted in static formulations in radical disharmony with modern conditions. Although there is no one Christian moral system such that the Christian faith depends on it, one of the outstanding characteristics of Christianity is precisely its moral character. The Christian faith stimulates, purifies, and elevates all the

---

[9] James Gustafson, "Context versus Principles: A Misplaced Debate in Christian Ethics," *Harvard Theological Review*, 58:2 (April, 1965), 192.

[10] C. F. D. Moule, "The New Testament and Moral Decisions," *The Expository Times*, 74:12 (September, 1963), 370.

moralities which mankind has developed in its long process of maturation.

Religious in its very roots, Christian morality springs from the response of man to the redemptive word of God. Christian life is one which flows from the victory of Christ, a life lived in anticipation of the second coming of Christ. Emphasis on the dynamic character of Christian morality will lead to a catechesis which presents it as the life of the spirit nourished in worship and in faith, an outgoing positive life of love. A cramped fear of wrongdoing is not characteristic of Christian moral living. Romans 8:2, the great declaration of Christian freedom, sets the tone for Christian moral catechesis. Christian moral life is life in Christ Jesus, and the spirit of this life is the spirit which makes moral teaching specifically Christian.

Toward a Totally Christian Moral Education

Christian education begins with the gospel. Confrontation with the word of God forces a man to a personal decision; either he lives out the consequences of the Christian message in his relationships with other men or he withdraws in selfishness thereby negating the message. In the first instance the constant tension between the individual and the community is a life-giving struggle; in the second, it is a death-dealing battle. Christian moral catechesis seeks to direct the struggle so that life rather than death eventuates.

Two dangers harass the conscientious catechist; he must carefully direct his efforts between two extremes. The first is the danger of legalism, the tendency to treat the gospel as a higher law. Legalism is not emphasizing the law to the exclusion of the gospel; rather, it is the effort to attain through the law the life that only the gospel can give. Legalism may creep into catechesis when students are not permitted to relate the gospel to the problems and situations of their daily life. The catechist may fall into the trap of setting up codes and identifying these, and only these, as Christian. Any overt or covert coercion which tempts the Christian to turn back to the works of the law as a means of gaining favor with God is legalism. Legalism effectively frustrates the work of the gospel.

A second danger lies in the tendency to advocate a morality that knows no restraints. Certainly, the Christian is the freedman of the Lord. As such, the law does not bind him. But even the Christian freedman needs nurture before he attains his destined maturity. Immediate, short-term sanctions to correct transgressions and to encourage effort are necessary to stimulate the growth of a truly interior morality. Basically, it is not a question of controlling actions by reason, or of practicing a particular virtue; it is rather question of acting as Christ would act, of loving with the same generosity and delicacy as he would love. Although the Holy Spirit guides the Christian so that he is led in fidelity, love, and confidence in a way which is worthy of a son of the eternal Father, this guidance does not occur magically. Guidance comes through human instruments. The way of Christian moral catechesis is to achieve a nice balance between the severity of legalism and the license of antinomism.

Only insofar as the Christian mystery is the source of thought and action can one speak of a moral education which is truly religious and Christian. Christian moral education renders a man more human, and growth in holiness makes a man ever more fully human. True Christian growth is always growth in faith, hope, and love, nothing less. Yet grace works through nature and pervades human life and conduct, leavening all. A man who responds to the world in a Christlike manner, who reflects at once the human and the divine: this is the goal of Christian moral catechesis.

Triple Dimension of Christian Morality

At baptism a new dimension enters man's ethical life. Referring to this phenomenon, Paul admonished the Ephesians to put on the new nature, created in the likeness of God in righteousness and holiness (Eph 4:24). The new ontological dimension, participation in the life of the Trinity, creates new potencies and brings new demands. This dimension has a triple face: faith, hope, and love are now the setting of the Christian's moral action. Each of these — faith, hope, and love — expresses the whole of Christian existence; each of them functions as the criterion of Christian moral living. This threefold totality is related to a basic fact of man's temporal existence.

Man lives in three dimensions of time. He lives in the past by memory and in the future by expectation; his existence in the present is something that he usually takes for granted. In his preoccupation with daily tasks the problematic character of his present existence usually escapes him.

The Christian lives in the past by faith; he lives in the future by hope; and he lives in the present by love. Each of these facets expresses the whole of the Christian existence.[11] All are equally essential and total because each expresses relation to Christ in a particular dimension of time.

Man's hope, the expectation of the full realization of God's will, has the same content as his faith, namely, Christ. Faith believes what hope expects, and hope expects what faith believes. But the real content of both faith and hope is the love of God revealed in Christ. Faith and hope are about God's love. They are nothing in themselves; they are something only in their relation to love. This is why Paul could affirm that the greatest of these is love. Love is the real substance of faith and hope. One cannot say that God is faith; he cannot affirm that God is hope, but he can say that God is love. Love is God's presence here and now in man. It is God's being as man's new being, his presence as man's own present. Although, in a certain sense, love divinizes man, it is only love in the sense of agápe that makes

---

[11] Emil Brunner, Faith, Hope, and Love (Philadelphia: The Westminster Press, 1956), p. 13.

him truly human. By Christ and in Christ the Christian is present with and to his brothers. In faith, hope, and love the Christian is drawn ever closer to God and to his fellowmen.

Paul did not consider faith, hope, and love as virtues; rather, he seemed to regard them as qualities of relationship. Although he was not primarily concerned with the regulation of life by rules of conduct, Paul constantly proclaimed an invitation to a relationship. In his writings one will not find a formulation of an ethical system with specific moral directives. The Holy Spirit, not a written code, gives the true answer to the demand for specific Christian rulings. Assuredly, however, in the Church, the community of Christians, the Spirit is active and God reveals himself. Within the Church God speaks in a plurality of sacramental signs, in the preaching of his word, in the inspiration of scripture, in the pronouncements of the magisterium. Here the Christian will find positive direction for translating into action the powers of faith, hope, and love which he received at baptism.

But acts of faith, hope, and love do not depend directly on external action. They come into existence without action and prior to action, but in time they are expressed in action. In eternity the inner act will attain fulfillment in the perfection of love while the objective realization in action will cease. In this life, however, faith, hope, and charity are both the work of God in man and man's answer to God's work.

The Contemporary Christian and the Call to Faith

Perhaps no Christian reality is so poorly understood as that of faith. Exaggerated emphasis on faith as an assent to a set of dogmas has resulted in a static conception of a dynamic reality.

Essentially, faith is personal encounter with God in Christ. evidence nor logical deduction leads to belief. Persons know Through the word of faith man is called to respond. Neither each other only through personal encounter and mutual self-manifestation. Since faith is an encounter with God, it comes only when God manifests himself to man. God reveals himself, he calls man, through human testimony. Transmitting the power, the life, and the joy which God gives him through faith, the Christian witness leads others to an ever deeper faith. There is an intimate connection between words and faith. In the epistle to the Romans (10:13–18) Paul suggests the relationship. By words God comes to meet man; in faith man answers God's call. Words can be regarded merely as signs which manifest another's thoughts; this is a static concept. However, words are also a summons because they are addressed to someone and tend to evoke a response; they reveal a speaker's interior attitudes and dispositions. Words tend to reveal the person. Revealing himself to his children through the words and acts of other Christians, God leads them to respond in faith to his call. But no created word or act is the ultimate ground of faith. Rather, the uncreated Word demands a free response. Divine ingenuity has arranged that the created should become the vehicle for the uncreated. Mystery this, but the result of divine-human cooperative action awakens a dialogue between God and man.

Normally, faith comes to the child in three ways: (1) through the life of the family and the parish; (2) through the word of God in scripture; (3) through systematic catechesis.[12] These three ways of faith are intimately related. The last flows from, and is subservient to, the other two. But systematic catechesis is not, for all that, unimportant. Indeed, it is a privileged way of transmitting the word of God which calls to faith in liturgy and scripture. Through the witness of doctrinal instruction as well as through scripture and liturgy, contemporary man hears the call to faith.

---

[12] Franz Schreibmayr, "The Faith of the Church and Formal Doctrinal Instruction," *Modern Catechetics*, ed. Gerard Sloyan (New York: The Macmillan Company, 1963), p. 45.

True, man is born to faith in baptism. However, catechesis plays a fundamental though not an absolute role in the transformation from potency to act. The particular efficacy of the catechetical act is due in no small part to the predisposition which the catechized has because of his baptismal consecration and to the proximate preparation for the assimilation of these truths in terms of the experiences of the early years.

Both catechist and catechized are immersed in the life of the Church. When they come together in a catechetical situation which is pervaded by a biblical, liturgical atmosphere, the Church, God dwelling among men, is also present. In this presence catechist and catechized are stimulated to a more open response to the word of God as encountered in scripture and sacrament. Thus, the catechetical action ends in liturgical worship, the expression in love of a full personal commitment to God. In the liturgy faith finds the complete expression for its love.

Faith and love are so inseparably related that one could well speak of a faith-love. The faith which acts through love is formed from two conjoined elements: the prompting of the Holy Spirit and the truths to be believed. The two are so intimately related that there is but one total work for the religious educator; while presenting the word of God he must foster a taste for God. Nurturing a living faith must accompany instruction. Nurture and instruction go together in somewhat the same manner as faith and love. Faith both leads to and flows from love, its center of gravity.

Love, Christian Center of Gravity

Love shifts the center of gravity from the self-centeredness of a merely physical life to the God-centeredness of a life in the spirit. Through the action of the spirit a new way of life opens out for man, a way where one walks buoyantly with the love of a son for his father and of a brother for his brothers. Christianity is essentially a message of love the first task of which is to reveal God's love to the world in the concrete form of effective brotherly love.

The religious and universal significance of the Christian message can be proclaimed only with difficulty if the Church appears to modern man as an institution that is closed and lives apart. This can happen if the Church seems too Western or gives the impression of being more interested in her social and cultural organizations than in the needs of humankind. Today's Christians must witness to the fact that Christianity is no mechanical or magical reality; it is a living witnessing that opens hearts for the message it brings. A self-contained, loveless Christianity would be a monstrosity. Christians must ever strive to become present to their fellowmen; they must constantly negate the image of the worried, self-centered follower of Christ. Essentially, the Christian task is to manifest the unity in diversity of Christian love.

Love is one; its different qualities belong together, although they may become isolated and antagonistic toward each other. Agápē without éros is cold obedience to a moral law; éros without agápē is chaotic desire which denies the validity of the other's claim to be acknowledged as an independent lovable and loving self. The unity of éros and agápē in the love of Christians is an implication of the Christian faith.[13] However, agápē is the determining factor in any conflict of the qualities of love; it transcends the finite limits of human love.

If éros is the motion of being drawn to, of being attracted by, agápē is the movement in the opposite direction. Agápē seeks to replenish the emptiness of the other; it does not seek to fill itself. Divine love knows no need; it is perfect in itself. God's love is entirely spontaneous, motivated only by his will to share; it is the consummate expression of his freedom. God is sharing, giving, self-communicating love; this is the mystery revealed in Christ.

---

[13] Paul Tillich, *Dynamics of Faith* (New York: Harper and Brothers, Publishers, 1957), p. 115.

In revealing a new kind of love in Christ, God has given men the power to express this love in a new way of life. The central ethical concern of the Christian is simply how to express this love in each moment of his existence. Love offers an unchangeable principle of ethics but its realization is dependent on continuous acts of a creative intuition. Love is above the law, but there is a certain degree of ambiguity in this statement. On the one hand, love is an unconditional demand; on the other hand, it is a power which breaks through all commands. It is just this ambiguous character of love that makes it the timeless solution to ethical questions in a changing world. Only love is able to appear in every existential moment or kairós. Law cannot because law is the attempt to impose what belongs to a special time on all times. Realizing itself from kairós to kairós, love creates a morality that is beyond the alternatives of absolute and relative ethics. Love is eternal, but it creates something new in each kairós. This revolutionary kind of love is the highest fulfillment of man's life because it grows out of the deepest revelation of the divine life. The Christian realizes his most creative possibilities when he loves with the redemptive love revealed and made available to him in Jesus Christ.

Through love and within love, in the life-giving coming together of brothers, the Christian realizes his potential. Love links those who love in bonds that unite but do not confound; love enables Christians to discover in their mutual contacts a power that is a reflection of the divine. In loving God and his brothers, the Christian assists the progress of the terrestrial synthesis of the Spirit. Precisely in the progress of this synthesis he draws ever closer to his brother while at the same time he ascends toward the Uncreated. Because he loves he finds himself constrained to participate in all the anxieties and all the aspirations of the earth. The catechetical task is to lead Christians from enclosed selfishness to open lovingness.

The man who totally loves the Father needs no commandments; for one who is so profoundly identified with Christ that it is Christ who thinks, wills, and loves in him, the law has no reason for being. Such a man has already been led from the enclosure of selfishness to the openness of love. However, such a perfect being does not exist on this earth; the abolition of all law would demand that the éschaton already be fully realized. Because of his terrestrial condition man needs some law; obedience to a commandment is the expression of his condition as creature. But this obedience is merely one aspect of the charity which impels him. The Christian law of love transforms all observances into means of responding to the divine love. Catechetical instruction will not take away all perplexity; rather, it will give indications that will implement this response in modern living.

In directing his students toward a synthesis of life which exemplifies a Christian response, the catechist may well follow the example of St. Paul. An examination of his letters reveals that the major portion was devoted to an exposition of the Christian identity in the mystery of the Church. Only when he had clearly delineated the Christian position did Paul give concrete corollaries in moral behavior. From the context of the Christian identity love expresses itself in the concrete situation. Paul's statements of moral cases were always presented as consequences of Christian love.

Following Paul's example, the catechist should help Christians to evaluate their position in their historical situation. An appreciation of their dignity and the responsibility which results from immersion in the Christian mystery will eventuate in a sharing, outgoing, self-communicating love. In the expression, Christian love will come to full maturity.

Hope, Christian Movement Toward Maturity

Man's baptismal covenant sets him on a new exodus; his is a partial victory ceaselessly inserted into the victory of Christ. The paradox of his existence is that the Christian is already born yet he must be born again each day. His existence is an existence in hope. Baptism is the passage from the state of sin to one of communion. The gradual development of this communion in all its fullness is the task of Christian hope.

Christian hope is no mere knowledge; it is an event. Expecting with joy a happy event, the Christian lives in the present for the future. However, the mystery of Christian expectation which is hope lies in the fact that the Christian already possesses in seed that for which he hopes. His very straining toward that which is to come frees him for the process of maturing, for a growing into the full stature of Christ. A bouyant youthfulness remains as the Christian attains his Christian maturity.

Through faith man is committed to a new way of life. But man does not enter this new life alone. In a mysterious way all creation shares in man's straining for the maturity which is his inheritance (Rom 8:12–39). So closely united is his destiny with that of his brothers — indeed, of all creation — that an isolated individualism has no place in the Christian existence. The whole of creation is turned toward this mystery in man, this interior becoming, struggling, and unfolding. It is a waiting, and the attention of this waiting is directed, not immediately toward God, but toward man, for man is the way creatures return to God.

The hope of the Christian is, therefore, both personal and universal. The love which man receives in faith gives him a worldwide perspective. A Christian cannot lead a merely private life; he is committed to God's work in the world. Thus, his personal hope has a universal aspect.

Perhaps there is no activity of the Christian life in which the double aspect of hope is so outstanding as in prayer. Prayer is the first movement of the new life, its breath, so to speak. In man the spirit himself longs for the consummation, and his longing is at once personal and universal. God's plan is a world plan, the perfection of his creation in the eternal kingdom. Therefore, the promise in Christ, the goal that is opened to him by faith as the content of hope, is world redemption. Individual salvation is merely the personal aspect of this greater hope. Catechesis on prayer should nourish the Christian expectation in its double aspect.

Christian hope is essentially communal. Not merely the expectation of an isolated individual, hope embraces the promises which the new people of God inherited from the chosen people. Although the eschatological and communal implications of this hope are too broad for human comprehension, Christian prayer should take this basic direction. Christian prayer should be directed to move confidently toward a final point at which a community of free men will be established.

In this process of maturation which is hope, let not the Christian forget that he must speak to God about his fellowmen. And in speaking to his fellowmen about God, perhaps he will have to speak in secular terms to be understood. This is one of the most important needs of the present age. Hope is a human prerogative; any terms which will implement the Christian movement toward maturity must not be despised.

From the vantage point of his faith in eschatological values already realized in the person of Christ, the Christian structures his own value system and directs his efforts toward realization in this world. Personal prayer, if it be truly Christian, inevitably leads to the eucharistic celebration where Christians commune with God and with one another.

In the eucharistic announcement of the death of the Lord until he comes (1 Cor 11:26) the Christian community and all creation moves toward the maturity which will be realized in the day of the Lord. Participation in the eucharistic feast brings the Christian to a mysterious accomplishment of a maturity toward which he still strives.

Catechesis should show the eucharistic banquet as a transforming sign of the consummation of an election which existed long before the law was born. The basic orientation of Christian moral catechesis will thus be universal and personal, temporal and supratemporal. In this elucidation of the mystery of the Christian expectation, the continuity as well as the discontinuity of the law will be more clearly delineated.

Outcomes of Christian Moral Catechesis

The covenant is not a treaty; it is a commitment, a way of living together which must be maintained in all the circumstances of life. God's commitment is irrevocable; man's is precarious. The law merely supplies the context within which the human commitment can be made more certain. But the law is also God's word, and like all of God's words, it nourishes. In his daily response to God's word the Christian exemplifies the continuous as well as the discontinuous aspects of the law.

Christian moral education begins with an evangelical confrontation. The gospel challenges men to live by the power of the spirit within the fellowship of the Christian community. It involves the individual as he makes his personal decisions, and its effects are seen in his relationships with his brothers. Now every human encounter becomes an encounter with God. Christian morality is thus theocentric, but not in a sense alien to man nor foreign to his world.

The community of Christians in the unity of Christ is an ideal; it is the image of the community as it ought to be according to the design of God. Although the Christian community in its earthly actuality is quite imperfect, the design is still recognizable and is imperceptibly being perfected. Personal union with Christ in the Eucharist effects a love-union among Christians which is not explainable in purely natural terms. This union reflects the divine love which is as extensive as it is intensive. In the growth of this love-union the mystery of Christ is ever more clearly revealed.

In his moral teaching the catechist must avoid both a false anthropocentrism and an inauthentic supernaturalism. The former would inculcate a purely human morality. To deduce norms of moral action from man himself is to give pre-eminence to the formation of good citizens. In such a system Christianity would be reduced to a series of beliefs and moral prescriptions. The latter extreme, a false supernaturalism, so emphasizes the radical nature of the Christian revolution that it places the Christian in a false opposition to the world. When man presupposes an absolute dichotomy between sacred and profane, he is likely to end in an irrelevancy somewhat akin to that of the Qumran sectaries in another aeon.

An authentic Christian moral teaching, however, places morality within its New Testament perspective of the response of man to the call of God. Showing the implications of this call demands that the catechist be always in touch with the modern world. A catechesis which shows the timeless nature of the divine imperative against the varied background of the contemporary situation is a seldom completely attained ideal.

Today's catechist must do what Paul did. Paul used the language and thought forms of Judaism to a considerable extent. On occasion he borrowed the language of the Greek world, but he often departed from both, modifying old ideas and producing new ones. Explaining the unknown by means of the known, Paul used whatever terms were available. He was not deliberately wedded to any one culture. If his language was largely judaic, it was because Jewish terminology was familiar to him, and this expression enabled him to deal with the subject matter in a way that his audience could understand. Both Judaism and Hellenism contributed vehicles for the transmission of Paul's message. When both failed, Paul coined new expressions to show the consequences of the new life in Christ. His ambition was to do no more than that.

The catechetical task must be freshly done in every generation, indeed in every new historical or personal situation. If contemporary moral catechesis would form a Christian who is truly a man of his time it must use the language of this century in much the same way that Paul used that of his era. This means that the catechist must courageously discard obsolete categories and seek contemporary expression for the Christian message. His proclamation, while mirroring the divine openness to the world, must explore creatively the situations in which modern man lives. Eminently practical, his catechesis will then lead Christians to a new realization of the personal and universal implications of the Christian law of love in their lives.

Love is the most fundamental maturing factor in life; a person's capacity to love is a direct measure of his maturity. Therefore, the aim of moral catechesis must be to help Christians grow in their ability to love. But only God can teach man to love. Historically, the Christ of the gospel pericopes is the clearest exemplification of the divine love. The catechist who highlights the various gospel incidents in which the divine manner of loving is translated into human actions in Christ will implement the divine educative activity. Christian moral catechesis must lead to the Eucharist, supreme expression in the present of divine love encountering human love.

Certainly Christian moral catechesis must enunciate norms. But norms can become meaningless abstractions. These norms are always to be evaluated in terms of that inner law of growth which traditionally has been called "natural law."[14]

---

[14] Louis Monden, *Sin, Liberty and Law*, translated by Joseph Donceel (New York: Sheed & Ward, 1965), p. 88. The complexity of the concept of natural law is reflected in Josef Fuchs, *Natural Law: A Theological Investigation*, trans. Helmut Reckter and John Dowling (New York: Sheed and Ward, 1965). On p. 30 Fuchs indicates that, while the natural law is not a positive law like the mosaic formulations, it is a commandment from without and not a power from within. However, on p. 32 Fuchs refers to it as the inner law of human morality emerging from the fact of human being. Until further studies prove the contrary, I would emphasize the objective but basically inward character of the natural law.

In the human community this law must be active, not merely as a norm deep within every human person; it must be made communicable, available as a principle of education and of community organization. Forever in a process of purification from all images in which a particular era or culture threatens to imprison it, this dynamic inner law serves as a norm for every change in its expression. Risk it certainly is, to express the changeless authenticity of the inner natural law in the language and conceptual forms of a new time, a new culture, a new attitude toward life. But this risk is a necessary catechetical task. Necessary, because the norm for Christian living is no longer mere human self-development but God's love which has penetrated man's innermost being through the Holy Spirit which has been given to him (Rom 5:5). In freely responding to the divine initiative in every situation the Christian does not only center his own love on the ultimate focus which is Christ. In his personal decision each Christian also commits his brothers and bears the responsibility of the decision of his time.

After the catechist has shown the concrete reality of Christian love in contemporary living, he must lead his students to the mystery of love as it is enacted, epitomized, expressed in the eucharistic sacrifice. When the Christian receives the sacramental touch of God, whose name is Jesus Christ, one may hope that he will grow in the realization that he only lives when he loves. With this realization the continuity as well as the discontinuity of the law will appear in proper perspective. In the eucharistic light the truth that God is love will be seen to be effectively summarized in the law of love. Only then will contemporary moral confusion tend to disappear.

CHAPTER V

LIBERTY, HALLMARK OF CHRISTIAN CONTEMPORARY LIFE

Mystery of Human Freedom

Liberty has always been an ambiguous battle cry. Man would be free, yet he is fearful, anxious in the face of freedom. Modern man frantically searches for a place where he can live with his newly won freedom but in his bewilderment and inability to bear the burden of liberty he tries to escape from his anxiety in work, in love, in restless activity. A fatalism born of weariness, loneliness, and fear threatens him.

Fearless freedom is a fruit of faith, a joyous hope which characterizes the mature Christian. And faith exists in time. Time is the proving ground of liberty, but time is ambivalent. On the one hand, it is destructive; it relegates everything into the past, to absence and non-being. On the other hand, time is creative; it brings the future to realization, the potential to actuality. Time is absence or presence, emptiness or plenitude, despair or hope. Human freedom determines whether the destructive or the creative aspect of time shall dominate. The Christian who freely responds to the divine call will find in faith support for a liberty which is always fragile and threatened.

Freedom *is* a burden. But a faith which looks toward love will enable man fearlessly to bear this mysterious burden in time. In eternity the burdensome character of liberty will disappear. But the mystery of human freedom will perdure.

Freedom is mystery indeed, a complex and awesome human prerogative. Modern man often fights for a freedom which he identifies with absolute autonomy. But the biblical ideal of freedom is quite different. Scripture deals with relationships, not concepts. A living God who frees captives, One in whom perfect freedom is embodied, a liberty to serve the creator: this is the multi-faceted image of freedom given in the scriptures.[1] Under divine guidance the Hebrews progressed from a primitive collectivism to an open personalism in which man stood before God in responsible personal dignity. Now biblical man was called in full freedom to enter into communion with God and to form a community with his brothers.

That freedom gives the opportunity to experience fulfillment through voluntary obedience to the will of God has never been generally understood or accepted. Even many Christians believe that there is a basic incompatibility between liberty and law. That this belief could easily arise in the first Christian century is not difficult to understand. Many of these Christians were converts from Judaism who had long borne the oppressive weight of ceremonial laws and legalistic interpretations. The bulk of these strictures dealt with circumcision, sacrifice, washings, cleansings, and meticulous observance of seasons of prayer and fasting. They had little or nothing to do with love, mercy, justice, the brotherhood of man, or the fatherhood of God. Therefore, it is not surprising that the early Christians welcomed release from such laws with an enthusiasm that led some to identify liberty with license.

However, modern man's definition of liberty in terms of release from all law, divine as well as human, is not so easily

---

[1] Suzanne de Dietrich, "Captives into Children: The Biblical Doctrine of Freedom," Interpretation, 6:4 (October, 1952), 389.

understood. Tending to interpret political and religious liberty in terms of absolute freedom from all law, modern man has thought of liberty as embodying the right of doing exactly as he wanted with little regard for the well-being of others. Aware at the same time of many obvious and subtle limitations upon his freedom, he struggles against biological, psychological, and cultural restrictions. While frequently knowing that he could (and perhaps should) have acted differently, man attempts to escape from guilt, responsibility, and even freedom. Paradoxically, however, the feeling of guilt is an assurance of freedom (albeit immature and limited) even when that freedom is denied.

Freedom is not always given antecedently, nor does it grow by steady development. Rather, man attains the freedom of Christian maturity by apparently fitful spurts of progression and regression. In the act of liberation the process of making choices is the reality, but the range of freedom in these choices admits of innumerable degrees. Between the extreme in which man can no longer do a wrong act and the other extreme wherein he has lost his freedom to right action, there are many degrees. Even in the life of a single man the degree of liberty can differ with each moment.

Gradually, but not steadily, human freedom reaches maturity. The gospel does more than free from the law, from sin, from death; it releases man from the constraints of guilt, from fear, from anxiety. To mature in freedom means to cast off the fear born of slavery and to discard the constraints of the slave for the freedom of the son. Liberty is the goal of the believer, but only a mature freedom is capable of full obedience, an obedience in which the person realizes himself most completely in his free surrender to another.

Paul earnestly commended freedom to Christians as their great task. However, he was always the realist, and he knew that the problem of freedom never would be simple nor easily solved. Always limited in scope by concern for the brother, Christian freedom would frequently be further limited by its very immaturity. Paul realized this; yet he ceaselessly urged Christians to work toward a full Christian liberation. The liberating struggle to become what he already is forces man to grapple with the limitations deriving from his immaturity. Christian freedom lies in Christ; all things are permitted provided they neither separate Christians from him nor harm the brother.

Limitation and Human Freedom

Immaturity, Crucial Problem of Freedom

Much has been written about modern man's coming of age. But the perceptive thinker soon comes to the conclusion that this heralded human maturation is not an accomplished fact. True, modern man strives desperately to be himself, and that self can be achieved only through freedom. But he wavers irresolutely between a striving for absolute autonomy and a retreat from the very liberty he prizes.

Man can bear many things, but he cannot bear unrelieved loneliness. Alienation is the soil which nurtures anxiety. The realization that the absolute autonomy for which he strives would only augment his isolation leaves modern man frightened, anxious. He seeks in vain to find himself in the lonely crowd where every other man is a faceless unit. Man only becomes truly man in a genuine meeting with his brothers. His impotence is his inability to give gifts.

True liberty involves gift-giving. The gift of oneself and the response of the other establishes that communion which liberates man for the freedom characteristic of maturity. The presence of the other is a constant reminder of the responsibilities that accompany mature freedom. Being present to the other also leads to liberation in maturity. Maturation is possible only in a community of persons; it is not possible in an aggregation of separated men whose only gift to one another is their common emptiness. In love Christian freedom fills this emptiness and bridges the separation.

True liberty is in no way related to caprice or arbitrariness. It does not consist in discarding all responsibility. Only one who risks total Christian self-giving will attain a truly responsible freedom. However, in his very acts of responsibility man frequently manifests something of the caprice of immaturity. Since freedom is a complex reality and the double aspect of liberation and determination is not readily distinguishable, one must look to the behavioral sciences for clarification of the ambiguity.

Insights of the Behavioral Sciences

Man is free; in a certain sense he is also determined. While Paul emphasized the former, he apparently did not advert to the truth of the latter. He considered human freedom in a generic manner. Most moderns still grapple with this twofold truth, and in a human manner tend to emphasize only one aspect. Perennial disputes regarding freedom tend to express the problem in such a way that it seems to be merely a psychological question. Could man also have refrained from an action? Could he have acted differently? Because human freedom is more than a psychological entity, exact and methodical verification of any answer to these questions is not possible.

The dialectic of freedom and determinism operates in every human action. Only this dialectic shows a freedom that is really human. Modern science finds more difficult the preservation of the moment of liberty than the discernment of the determining factors in man's activity.

Nevertheless, behavioral sciences have pointed the way to a new and deeper appreciation of the mystery of liberty. A consideration of the divergent viewpoints of Sigmund Freud and Alfred Adler may throw further light on the modern crisis of freedom and also give a deeper insight into the nature of human freedom.

Freudian Deterministic Emphasis

Accepting no human activities as accidental, Freud was the first to apply the principle of causality to the study of personality in the form of a literal and uncompromising psychic determinism.[2] His predecessors did not doubt that all events were caused, but they distinguished between those for which the cause could be readily postulated and those which were the result of many separate and apparently trivial causes which it would be (as they thought) impossible to analyze. Freud's predecessors held that most psychological happenings were in the latter group and therefore could be discussed only in broad descriptive terms.

Freud disagreed with this older interpretation of psychological determinism. His early studies of hysterical patients showed that the apparently irrational symptoms which had puzzled physicians could be understood when seen as expressions of painful memories which had been repressed into the unconscious.[3] A logical continuity in the mental life of the individual became evident, and abnormal symptoms were seen as revealing specific individual stresses which caused exaggerated expressions of processes common to everyone.

Freud did not postulate a simple one-to-one relationship of cause and effect in all psychic events, but he did believe all behavior to be motivated and goal-directed. He pointed out that there are no fortuitous psychological expressions; character traits, errors, slips of the tongue, and memory lapses: all were caused by some past event.[4] Only obliquely did he treat the problem of human freedom; however his stand for an historical, instinctual determinism out of the subjective past had far-reaching implications for human liberty.

Freud's belief that the person was a social atom which

---

[2] Sigmund Freud, *An Autobiographical Study*, trans. James Strachey (London: Hogarth Press, 1946), p. 86.

[3] Sigmund Freud, *The Problem of Anxiety*, trans. Henry Alden Bunker (New York: The Psychoanalytic Quarterly Press, 1936), p. 85.

[4] Freud, *An Autobiographical Study*, p. 85.

required community only as a means for the satisfaction of needs, and his conception of a basic hostility so strong that only sheer necessity or common hatred could join people in love, resulted in a limited conception of human possibilities for real communion. Likewise, his mechanistic view of man tended to compartmentalize him and thus to reduce mutuality. Characteristic Freudian emphasis on the past as cause for the present and determinant for the future seemed to limit responsibility. The degree of mutuality involved in a human act is a necessary consideration in determining the degree of freedom shown in any human action.

Freud viewed the infant as a mass of impulses lacking in any directing consciousness. In the child's coming to terms with external reality Freud saw a part of the primeval conglomeration becoming differentiated as the ego or self. Later, through the need to face the moral prohibitions of society, the superego develops.[5] The superego is only partly conscious; this explains the guilt feelings that an individual may experience after performing an action which rationally he knows is not in the least immoral. Freudian theorists would seem to imply that the supergo is a powerful force, a force which is neither instinctual, somatic, nor a completely external reality, but which nevertheless impinges upon human freedom.

Although unconscious forces do not necessarily negate the active, self-determining function of the will, their influence may diminish both the degree of freedom and the moral value of the act. Knowledge and acceptance of the determining forces in the human personality do not necessarily mean a denial of other human powers. Indeed, far from being opposed to freedom, psychic determinism is regarded by some psychologists as a necessary step or condition for its acquisition.[6] Whether an act is free or deter-

[5] Cf. Sigmund Freud, *The Ego and the Id*, trans. Joan Riviere (London: The Hogarth Press, Ltd., 1949), pp. 86 ff.

[6] Noel Mailloux, "Psychic Determinism, Freedom, and Personality Development," *Canadian Journal of Psychology*, 7:1 (March, 1953), 8.

mined will depend on the way dynamic factors within the individual release the activity. An action will not be free when the motive forces cause a chain-like reaction, materially determined by natural process. On the other hand, when the individual faces motives as value-elements which he recognizes without being completely absorbed by them, he will act freely.

No new problem is raised by the fact that certain tendencies derive from the unconscious. Acceptance of the instinctive elements in human nature can constitute an important step in the increase of the human power of freedom. As he understands better the determining forces in his nature, a man can become capable of new creative liberty in decision and action. Thus freedom, that mysterious blend of liberty and necessity, is seen less as an enigma and more as a characteristic of the mature personality.

Adlerian Indeterministic Emphasis

Alfred Adler also defended psychic determinism. However, in contrast to Freud's historical determinism out of the subjective past, Adler stood for an ahistorical determinism out of the subjective future.

As a result of serious differences with Freud, Adler in 1910 broke with the movement and founded a system based on the thesis that human behavior can be explained in terms of a struggle for power, a struggle designed to overcome feelings of mental or physical inferiority. According to Adler, the lever of psychological development was to be found in the feeling of inferiority. The increasing number of ethical imperatives felt by the child augmented his feeling of inferiority, and the stronger the feeling of inferiority the more violent was the ensuing reaction. Making external demands his own, the child replaced imperatives of compulsion by imperatives of freedom. In maintaining himself as independently willing, the individual removed painful pressures, overcame inferiority feelings, and became master of himself.[7]

Adler's immanent teleology implied ultimate indeterminism. Even the child, he believed, worked in a realm of freedom with his own creative power.[8] He was convinced of the free creative power of the individual in earthly childhood and of the restrictions imposed once the child had developed a fixed law of movement for his life. While admitting influences of the environment, Adler denied that these influences provided the basis for predicting future actions. Adler believed that each individual's judgment of himself represented his freedom of choice which was directed toward molding the pressures that heredity and environment had exerted on him. This limited freedom, he maintained, was a spark of individuality which manifested the physical, intellectual, and psychological uniqueness of each person.[9]

Adler pointed out that man is ruled by his purposes regardless of whether or not they are recognized by him. Although he acknowledged that emotions were the nervous energy that sparked human activity, Adler denied that they were the causes of human actions. While admitting that emotions aid man's real purposes, Adler would not concede their power to dictate. Emotions do not have an autonomous life; they are created by man and must follow his ultimate purpose. Thus he claimed that goals rather than objective historical factors were ultimate determinants of individual behavior.

Even Adler's disciples note, however, that his extreme indeterministic statements should be discounted as pragmatic expediences. There is a growing conviction that free behavior, far from being unpredictable, is most predictable.

---

[7] Heinz and Rowena Ansbacher (eds.), *The Individual Psychology of Alfred Adler* (New York: Basic Books, Inc., 1956), p. 147.

[8] Alfred Adler, *Social Interest: A Challenge to Mankind*, trans. John Linton and Richard Vaughan (London: Faber and Faber, Ltd., 1938), p. 191.

[9] G. Margery Allen, "The Adlerian Interpretation of Compulsion," *Essays in Individual Psychology*, ed. Kurt Adler and Danica Deutsch (New York: Grove Press, Inc., 1959), p. 55.

But it is not predictable in the same way as behavior resulting from a deterministic process or a repetition compulsion. When confronted with a problematic situation, the man who is truly free is the only one who is completely reliable; his behavior is predictable because he alone is capable of making and executing the right choice. While on the one hand one can be certain that this man will do the right thing, on the other hand, such an achievement escapes the outsider's prevision as any genuine discovery.

Adler's deep insights — his awareness of the personality as a unity, of the significance of non-sexual factors, of the part played by the ego, of the importance of cultural factors, and of the responsible character of true human love — advanced the understanding of that unique human prerogative, liberty. From the privileged historical situation of the second half of the twentieth century the polarity of the Adlerian and Freudian positions can be seen to have produced a more mature comprehension of the mystery of human freedom. Incidentally, advances in the behavioral sciences have brought a new and deeper understanding of sin. Now sin can be seen not only as an indication of human freedom, but also as a limiting of that freedom.

Sin, Expression and Limitation of Freedom

The Christian conception of freedom strikes a middle course between determinism and indeterminism. In positing man's responsibility before God, scripture presupposes human liberty. On the other hand, man's status as creature definitively limits his freedom. The apparently ambiguous character of Christian independence is rooted in its dependency. Paradoxically, man attains liberty in direct proportion to his dependence on God. And his very effort to free himself from dependence on God leads him into bondage. In attempting to prove his freedom by emancipating himself from God, man ends by surrendering his liberty.

Man's situation is still more complicated by the fact of

sin. Man is no longer whole; he is born a sinner. The core of sin in man is a fundamental individualism which causes him to make use of all for his own petty and immediate purposes. The man who sins performs an essentially ambivalent action. In striving toward a good, he goes against God's covenant and law. Thus sin is negative, but its denial becomes concrete in a positive action. Even the most direct hardening against God and one's brothers remains a self-affirmation, a positing of freedom.

Assuredly, sin involves self-destruction; however, first and foremost, sin is rather a breaking of the covenant. It is life in covenant, a life of personal communion, which man freely rejects when he sins. The rupture of the covenant brings the penalty of death.

A certain duality, akin to that present in sin, is also evident in death. Death is something which the individual must undergo, but it is also an act of man proceeding from within. This duality makes death essentially obscure. It is the penalty and the expression of sin; it is also the climax of sin. In the foregoing sense death limits man's freedom. Concomitantly, however, death is the final expression of human freedom. In death man can utter his highest word of love or he can commit the sin which is fully *anomía*, sin unto death, sin against the Holy Spirit.

Scripture records the fact that very soon after creation man used his freedom to sin. Partaking as it does in some of the ambiguity of the sinful act, death is, in a certain sense, a correlative of sin. The warning of the penalty of death (Gen 2:17) should be understood as meaning that death (not instant death, however) would follow sin. What is decreed as punishment for sin is not any kind of death, but a death of separation which is figuratively described as a return to dust. Likewise in Genesis, chapter three, death is connected with the state of alienation from God. Much later, in the epistle to the Romans (1:32; 6:16; 7:5; 8:6, for example) Paul presented death as the final result of sin. In 1 Cor 15:56 Paul depicted death as the last foe which Christ must destroy at his return. Certainly, the context includes bodily death, but the concept also embraces death as a sign of alienation from God.

The sinful misuse of human freedom has highlighted two seemingly irreconcilable principles which emerge in the biblical view of history. Scripture affirms God's sovereignty; all history fulfills his providential purposes. Yet, in a certain sense man also determines history. How can man be truly free in an order which fulfills the divine purposes? Completely deterministic as well as totally voluntaristic explanations must be rejected by the Christian who affirms both divine providence and human freedom.

However awkwardly he has manifested it, the history of salvation shows man repeatedly attempting to express his freedom through sin. Paradoxically, however, this very act which expresses human liberty so dramatically also effectively binds man. Although the action of his free will is restricted, even in his sinful situation man retains freedom of choice. Thus he remains guilty in his liberty, and because of his freedom of will his liberty is a real bondage. Existentially, human freedom is always bound and limited, but the binding and limiting results not from an impairment of free will. It results from the situation in which man stands or which he himself brings about. The expression of his liberty becomes, in the act of sinning, a real bondage. Just as bondage is the quintessence of sin, so liberation is the quintessence of life in Christ.

Characteristics of Christian Freedom

The freedom of the children of God is the fundamental kērygma of the Christian gospel (Rom 8:17). In contrast to the personal autonomy of the Stoics, Christian liberty is qualitative rather than quantitative. The contemporary crisis of freedom is an identity crisis. Freedom is intimately linked with the mystery of the individual name of each person. In his struggle to achieve self-identification man likewise strives to identify the freedom for which he longs. Like other Christian mysteries, freedom resists analysis. However, perhaps three characteristics best identify freedom as Christian. True Christian freedom is loving; it is responsible; it is communal.

Characteristic Christian Love

In the Christian community of love man acquires the highest freedom. Christian freedom is not a liberation from the bonds of nature; it is rather a liberation from solitude and the limitations of an individualistic self-love. The Christian reaches a fulfillment which is the expansion of his whole being in a perfect freedom of love. In loving his brother for himself, the Christian mysteriously, but nonetheless really, loves God incarnated in him. Like a disincarnate freedom, a disincarnate love would be an illusion. Incarnated in Jesus Christ, God's freedom is his freedom to love.

Because men are free, they cannot reach fulfillment without love. The fundamental power of love (the force of the love of God, of others, of himself in God) constitutes the person. For liberty is above all a power of spontaneous gift from one person to another; it is love. Man has a twofold freedom. In addition to his free will, there is in the depths of man a fundamental liberty of existential and totalizing option. This fundamental option, this existential and total engagement in love, must be actualized in concrete situations. Essential human liberty is expressed in daily actions; it becomes incarnate in human situations.

Wherever there is freedom, situations arise which cannot be covered by the letter of the law. A more dynamic directive is needed. That directive is love. Love is insight into circumstance; much more exactly than law, love freely determines the morality of the situation. The way of Christian love must be freely chosen. Even if they are forced to go through the motions of love, no external power can compel people to love one another. Christian love exists only in an atmosphere of liberty and of joyful responsibility. A real dependence and a very real independence character-ize the Christian law of liberty. Christian love makes man free in the exact measure in which he depends on the object of his love; he is captive in the exact measure in which he depends on that which he cannot love. In loving the other, the Christian consecrates his profound freedom. Any friend-ship, any total gift of oneself in love implies a risk and com-mitment which far surpasses the demands of external law. In the personal giving of himself to the other the Christian transcends the colorless precision of the law to penetrate intuitively into the sphere of faith and love.

The beginning of the epistle to the Colossians reveals a man who loved and was not afraid to express his love. For Paul liberty was not license nor the opportunity for the pro-motion of selfish personal interests. Rather, Christian liberty was an opportunity to serve others in love and thus to bring them to the freedom which man can find only in Christ. Paul glorified in the liberty which came to him in Christ. But he also realized that this freedom is always a call to love. A love that is unconditionally given, a love that is fully responsible: this is the love that fulfills the law.

Freedom in Responsibility

Although no intrinsic difference distinguishes modern man from his forebears, a greater sense of responsibility would seem to characterize him. As he has gained greater mastery over material elements, a deep change has occurred in man. His increasing independence has enabled him more effectively to respond to God as father. Not that he has always done so! But his coming of age in a secular world has brought with it a focalization (albeit unconscious) of the meaning of his inheritance. To be capable of responding freely to another, man must be independently and responsibly engaged in the world.[10]

Christ's cosmic victory over satanic powers has brought a progressive liberation from the forces in a culture which cripple and corrupt human freedom. No longer do these forces have the power to determine man; now man has the power and responsibility to rule over them. God's action in Christ calls man to a life of freedom from and responsibility for all creation.

As man has achieved a more mature relationship with the world, the power of the law over him has diminished. But his growing freedom has brought a danger. Because he is free, man can always surrender his freedom; once again he can enslave himself to the powers. Only if he freely chooses it, can man realize Christian liberation. If he answers the divine call to freedom, he must realize that this is at the same time a call to responsibility.

This fusion of freedom and responsibility is enunciated in the biblical symbol of sonship. A key passage in understanding the Christian's relationship to the world is Galatians 4:1 where Paul begins a discussion of man's coming to maturity. Basically, Paul's message is that now man can be free if he chooses. But responsibility is a necessary correlative of Christian liberty. Concretely, this means that Christians must stop attributing social injustices and family strife, for example, exclusively to economic forces and psychological pressures. They must grapple responsibly with the problems of the world.

Truly, man has come of age. But his freedom from the world depends upon his ability to take responsibility for it. The Christian is a son of God, but to come into his inheritance he must advance toward the status of the adult offspring who gradually assumes the role once played by his father. The timidly immature man retreats from responsi-

---

[10] Friedrich Gogarten, *The Reality of Faith*, trans. Carl Michalson and others (Philadelphia: The Westminster Press, 1959), p. 55.

bility; childishly he shakes off obligations. The mature Christian binds himself in freedom and freely maintains this binding. The man who acknowledges no obligations is not free; he acts impulsively and confuses freedom with license. True Christian liberty is not merely freedom *from*; it is also freedom *to*. It is the ability to respond personally and freely to the claims of God and his brothers. Full responsibility is characteristic of the mature Christian freedman. Often the immature man can only react, and this reaction is frequently automatic, blind, irresponsible. The mature Christian, on the other hand, does not *have* a response; he *is* that response. One of his capabilities is that of responding in a completely human manner to the demands of each situation.

The Christian has a responsibility in love which he cannot evade; his brother is for him an inescapable responsibility. A pressing task in Christian education is the communication of gospel morality in such a way that it is seen as a witnessing to fellowship in the Holy Spirit. Catechists must clearly show that the law of Christ is at once a law of freedom and a law of solidarity. A certain tension between the aspirations of the individual and the needs of the community will always exist. Christian freedom takes responsibility for harmonizing the two. Christian freedom in the fellowship of the Holy Spirit gives a joyous responsibility that is not stifled by trivial legalities and distrust. In freely responding to his environment the Christian fulfills himself and helps to bring fulfillment to his brothers.

Increased emphasis on responsibility in discussions of morality augurs well for the future of Christian moral teaching. Stress on man's right to determine in responsible freedom the correct course of action has resulted in less dependency on the prefabricated solutions of experts in casuistry. In the past exaggerated dependence upon casuistry has betrayed Christians into trusting in the law rather than the gospel. Law without gospel is arbitrary and abstract; it cannot discriminate among cases. Assuredly, principles are indispensable in moral teaching, but too often more emphasis on principles results in less emphasis on persons. After all, Christ died to save people; he did not die to preserve principles. Exaggerated emphasis on principles has resulted in a travesty of the Christian message, the atheism of legalism, which has made Christianity seem irrelevant to the modern world.

The moral action of the Christian is not merely a matter of affirming oneself in isolation; it is self-affirmation in relation to the other. The Christian law of freedom is one which affirms the community. Practically, this means that actions which maintain and promote the community are right; those are wrong which disrupt and jeopardize it. The mature Christian seeks the good of the community; his openness and responsiveness to the other fulfills the law of love which has as goal a living and vital relationship with the other as other. Personal responsibility thus implies the continuity of oneself in the community of persons to whom the response is given. The Christian's actions are a confident movement toward the final point at which the community of free men will be fully realized.

Rapidly changing sociological conditions of modern life accent the need for a communally-oriented moral catechesis. Responsible moral teaching educates Christians in their vocation to love, in their call to freedom. That freedom can be Christian only insofar as it is communitarian is an urgently needed catechetical emphasis.

Freedom in Community

A pure freedom of independent individuals, each concerned only with exploiting the other or organized into groups to achieve this purpose more effectively, would be an anomaly; it would be a denial of the covenant. By its very nature Christianity calls man to seek himself in the other and to trust that in the other he will encounter himself in an ever-increasing fulfillment. The divine elective action, creating a community in which men are freed from one another in such a manner that they assume responsibility for one another and are bound together as one, is the dialectic of Christian freedom.

The word of God is always creative; it always communicates love. The divine encounter brought by God's word invites men to live in love. And to live in love means to live in openness to one's brothers. Love cannot, without ceasing to be love, fail to require a real at-one-ment. The breach which makes fellowship impossible must be filled up. Love is will to fellowship. Atonement consists in the fact that the divine love, God's Word, took upon himself the task of bridging the gap which man's selfishness had made. In the paschal act that bridged the gap the Christian community was born.

The Christian community finds fulfillment in the eucharistic action. As a community the Church has the responsibility of acknowledging its dependence upon the Father's love. In the act of eucharistic worship the individual in community of faith most fully engages his Christian being in glorifying the creator. In the eucharistic situation the human power of loving is challenged to its depths by confrontation with infinite love. Mysteriously, in the reciprocal love of his brothers the Christian responds most adequately to divine love. The most vibrant expression of love incarnate, the eucharistic action of God's people is at the same time the most effective education in Christian livng.

Christian life requires a living out of the implications of the situation of the Lord's freedman. Since the Christian lives in community, and since it is only in community that he can come to a realization of his status of freedom, it follows that if education is to be Christian it must be an education to and for freedom in community. A communitarian, responsible love is the essence of Christian freedom. It is also the aim of religious education.

Education for Christian Freedom

The truly educated individual is a free person. To have liberty is not the same as to be free. The former is a possession, whereas the latter is a process, a function. Although freedom tends to express itself exteriorly, it is not bound to external situations. Freedom is an attitude toward oneself in relation to the world, a projection of oneself into the world. It is a dynamism that allows movement between persons; one can be free only in interdependence. Fulfilling man's natural bent, Christianity calls him to an adventure in unity in which he frees himself by joint action with others. Christianity stands for freedom, a responsible freedom of people bound together in a personal order of love.

At the level of scholarship psychological investigation has negated an ideal freedom, the disincarnate morality of the nineteenth-century manuals. However, the level of scholarship has not yet completely penetrated the level of practice. Disincarnate freedom seems to be the conventional wisdom passed on to this generation of Catholics. Too often in a typical catechetical situation a group of children beset by an unbelievable variety of determinisms is trained chiefly in sins and non-sins. These children are unrealistically expected to use these sins and non-sins as determinants for the morality of acts they will not be called upon to accept or reject for several years.

The dangerous illusion of a disincarnate freedom, one which supposes a vacuous area in which the quality exists, breeds disillusion, a disillusion that comes from treating people as automatons. Usually by the time they reach later adolescence the majority of children educated under such a system become well-adapted conformists, albeit on a superficial level. Those among them who feel this superficiality as emptiness sometimes revolt against their depersonalization in the interests of law. Truly, the imposition of such a moral system is a travesty of Christian freedom.

True Christian liberty presupposes at least a modicum of psychological freedom. The demands of morality may not be compromised, but the educator must see freedom as it exists in persons; human freedom is always limited. People vary in their ability to love, but the ability to love is a symptom of the ability to act freely. The catechist who wishes to educate for freedom must, therefore, develop the ability to love.

The first step in educating for Christian liberty is the guidance of the child away from insistence on the sovereignty of his own ego to a willingness for cooperation with others. In the process the educator must give as much freedom of movement and initiative as possible. A basic pedagogical principle is that the educator must lead his pupil to a point where he lives so excellently that the educator's intervention is finally unnecessary. Always, the catechist's love must respect, demand, and foster the other's freedom.

The catechist must remember, however, that real liberty stands at the end of education not at the beginning. Perhaps the most delicate task in education is making certain that the growing dialogue of dependence and autonomy takes place as harmoniously as possible. Premature casting aside of the restraints of the law leads to bewilderment and helplessness. Even in the best-planned program, however, crises will occur when the individual's capacity for autonomy falls short of the impassioned will for liberty. In these moments the young Christian may rebel against all external restrictions. These are the times when the catechist must patiently lead his students toward an exercise of responsible freedom through a conscious articulation of the meaning of their existence and mature response to present situations.

Essentially, freedom is freedom to love. Any limitations on freedom are also limitations on the ability to love. In the catechetical situation Christians must experience freedom. They must see freedom in action. Then they will know it. And the knowledge will make them free. In freedom they will love.

Election, the Law, and Covenantal Freedom

Election in Historical Perspective

Love originated not with man but with God. Already in creation God elected man, he chose man to participate in the divine activity of loving. But in communicating his elective love to man, God acted in time. As they developed through specific geographical, historical, and sociological factors, God chose a particular people. The land, the climate, a series of historical events: in successive generations these factors worked to forge a people capable of corresponding with the divine love.

Gradually, the conviction grew that the Hebrews were a chosen, an elected people. The doctrine of the election of the Jews was not decided in a moment; it was developed over a period of more than a thousand years. Basically historical, the divine election was not simply a divine decision communicated to Abraham or Jacob. By degrees the Jews understood that their history provided the basis for the fundamental idea of the chosen people. The central claim of election was not that God objectively favored the Jews above all other people but that he revealed himself most clearly through them.

At least as early as the third millennium B.C. the suzerain-vassal concept was deeply impressed on the social and political thinking of the ancient Near East. To some extent this was an extension of a primitive belief that covenants of some kind were essential for peaceful coexistence of varied social groups. In its most elementary sense a covenant was an agreement between two parties. Its most apparent aspect, its contractual character, was not, however, its most profound meaning, for the binding force of the covenant was psychic community.[11] Not primarily a juridical term, a covenant was in essence a mutual commitment or promise of fidelity which

---

[11] J. A. Thompson, "The Near Eastern Suzerain-Vassal Concept in the Religion of Israel," *The Journal of Religious History*, 3:1 (June, 1964), 1.

established a new community of life between the covenanting parties. Within the covenant community the individual realized a unique relationship with the sovereign, one which simultaneously bound in fidelity and freed from fear of reprisal. In view of Israel's deep involvement in a suzerain-vassal environment, it is not surprising that she came to understand her relationship with Yahweh in similar terms. The fact that the Near Eastern treaty pattern featured so strongly in the Exodus-Sinai event has been taken as evidence that Moses first made use of the suzerain-vassal metaphor to express the idea of Yahweh's sovereignty over Israel. Certainly, the treaty pattern influenced the literary form of many Old Testament passages which describe the Sinai covenant and the earliest covenant renewal ceremonies in Israel. Deuteronomy, the Old Testament covenant document *par excellence*, is cast in the form of the treaty pattern. Regardless of the date of its final composition, Deuteronomy points back to an original event in which Israel entered into a covenant with Yahweh in the land of Moab.

Each part of the literature of the torah bears the stamp of its own age and the mark of its inevitable limitations. At the same time, however, every page of this literature proclaims that the torah is the living word of God concretized in the covenantal contract. Behind the various legal codes and narratives the elected people felt the impact of God's love, the momentum of a revelation which freed them in covenantal love. Ordinarily, love cannot be commanded. But the divine election revealed God's longing for human reciprocation; the revelation demanded the response of human love. Commanded and yet free, the human response in love to the divine call became man's covenant commitment.

For a reason that was never clear to Israel, Yahweh had chosen her to cooperate with him in fulfilling his purposes in the world. In freely accepting the covenant, Israel had bound herself to observe the law as the constitution of her society. The metaphor of the suzerain-vassal relationship gave expression to Israel's situation in a most vivid and concrete way. Yet it was only a metaphor. The relationship between Yahweh and Israel was deeper than any legal contract could define. The religious relationship between Yahweh and Israel involved a reciprocal faithfulness of a kind that was unknown among the suzerains and vassals of the ancient Near East. The suzerain-vassal metaphor only gave formal and concrete expression to the more fundamental elements of election and commitment.

Election in Present and Future Perspective

Time is the peculiar feature of the present aeon. Best described in an adjectival sense, time is the attribute of the world in which man lives. It is a moving toward the end. Eternity is not the opposite of time; the opposite of time is the end. Time and eternity are neither parallel nor contiguous; expressed in terms of motion, they move on different planes. The horizontal line which is time and the vertical line which is eternity intersect whenever man hears God's word; in this eternal irruption into time the end becomes perceptible.[12] God's word, spoken in history, is sign of the divine election.

All men, living on the horizontal line of history, experience the tension between time and eternity. But the Christian is more vulnerable to the disruption of eternity. His degree of openness to the fact of the incarnation determines his sensitivity to the clash of time and eternity. To stand in fidelity to the divine word is always to stand in the dialectic between time and eternity.

Chosen in time, man was elected with reference to the messiah; in him rebellious man was metamorphosed into an obedient son. Indeed the New Testament knows of no other election except in Christ Jesus. All that Christians do, they do in the name of Jesus Christ.[13] In no act is this so evident

---

[12] Jakób Jocz, *A Theology of Election: Israel and the Church* (London: S.P.C.K., 1958), p. 167.
[13] See Col 3:12–17.

as it is in the Christian liturgical action. Concretization of the divine election in the present, the Christian's liturgical doing in Christ Jesus is simultaneously presage of the future. Thus, the liturgy is at once sign and actualization of a temporal election which is also eternal.

Christian baptism is an inchoative form of the new covenant relationship into which the Christian enters fully in the eucharistic action. In offering the eucharistic sacrifice the Church, the community of redeemed who have been elected in Christ, continues to place the covenant action for Christ and to enter more deeply into the covenant. In a more profound manner than the Israelite community, the Christian community in the celebration of Christ's paschal action enters into the covenant commitment of the chosen people of God.

In the eucharistic covenantal action Christians share mutually with Christ and with one another the responsibility of the covenant pattern, and the covenant pattern is love. By assembling together, by eating of the same bread and drinking of the same cup, Christians discover the meaning of personal, face-to-face love of brother. Especially in the Eucharist, the Church is a unifying community amidst the divisions and alienations of history. It is the union of an elected people; it is election actualized in the history of the redeemed community. In the Eucharist the Christian knows that he has been loved from all eternity in the eternal Son. And he realizes ever more fully that his own vocation is grounded in this eternal election.

Because the Eucharist is the new covenant, it is likewise the most forceful sign of divine election. In eucharistic action the Christian community is confronted with divine elective action in a living and present from. The Eucharist is the supreme challenge to respond to the divine vocation to love. At the same time, the eucharistic action is also the Christian community's answer to God's invitation to friendship. Supreme and fulfilling action of the Christian community, the Eucharist is also the human response to the divine election.

Freedom and Election

The Hebrew concept of freedom did not rest on an ideal human self-sovereignity as did the Greek idea. The hebraic ideal of freedom depended on a social relationship with the Lord of the covenant. Although the Hebrew's very dependency on Yahweh liberated him in a way the Greek ideal never could, nevertheless both Hebrew and Greek needed rebirth to a new freedom. Christian baptism is the rebirth to the freedom of the sons of God. As members of the risen Lord, Christians now stand before God in the freedom of sons; their Christian covenantal status is the condition for which the chosen people longed.

Essentially, this elected people is constituted on the basis of contact between two freedoms: the loving freedom of God who chooses his people, and the freedom of man who responds to God in love. Historically, the union of the two freedoms gave birth to the chosen people, a people freely committed to express its election in covenantal love. When the chosen people rescinded the covenant a new people was elected. The Church, originating in an encounter between human and divine freedom, is prime expression of the divine electing love. In the mysterious union of freedoms the Spirit takes hold of man. Indeed, election is a mystery of freedom.

In the present the mystery of freedom must be lived out on the level of worship. Liberation from evil, the Eucharist is also the supreme example of the way men are to attain freedom in love. The Eucharist teaches the most basic law of Christianity: man becomes free by loving.

Election, the End of the Law

The time has come to reiterate the truth that the law can be understood only within the context of the covenant, and ultimately, of election. In the aura of election the continuity as well as the discontinuity of the law is exemplified.

Paul's message of the Christian's radical freedom from the law depends upon the parallel statement that Christ is the end of the law. Christ did not merely mediate the new covenant. He is that covenant. He is the new law.

Thus, freed from the letter of the law, the Christian is liberated in its spirit. Although the divine election is apparently abrogated in its temporary rejection by the Jews, it mysteriously continues through time into eternity. Freed from external law, the Christian fulfills his election in the inner law of the spirit. In the divine election is found the key to the mystery of the law. Election is the beginning of the law. Election is also the law's end.

Modern man is not called to be faithful to the law; he is called to be faithful to a person. He does not need a legal formula to be repeated mechanically; he does need the good news of his election in Christ. Sign of love, this election is also sign of liberation. The law, too, is sign of love. In a deep though less obvious sense the law is also mark of freedom.

In fidelity to the new law, Christian catechesis must spell out the implications of divine electing love. Only thus will man's free commitment to divine love progress, and the law have reached its end.

APPENDIX

SOME BACKGROUND FOR PAUL'S TEACHING ON THE LAW

Throughout the Old Testament God providentially guided men in a progressive understanding of the law. Paul's concept of the law was inextricably united with that of the Old Testament. And the Old Testament concept was no simple entity. Although the law was a constant in the history of salvation, it was by no means a static concept. Israelite history reveals first one, then another, aspect of the entity. At one time the law was understood to include the whole of revelation — all that God had made known of his nature and all that he would have men be and do. Under one aspect torah was the vehicle; in another and deeper view it was the whole content of revelation.

From a natural point of view, the law was the expression of a conservative process, the holding of old laws as norms, and the evolution of new legal forms to meet the developing situations of a more complex society. However, through all vicissitudes and sometimes pathological interpretations, the law always retained something of its uniquely God-given dynamic element; mysteriously, it pointed beyond itself to an indefinite day of fulfillment. This Old Testament perspective is essential for an understanding of the fulfillment which Paul proclaimed.

Moral Education during the Exile

The Babylonian exile brought certain fundamental changes in the religious life of Israel; soon a crisis of faith developed. The kingdom was gone; the people was uprooted. The question: "What is Israel's destiny now?" clamored for an answer. The necessity the exiles had of preserving their faith even when deprived of temple worship led them to a reappraisal of their tradition and to a new stress on the law.

133

The exilic priestly community devoted itself to intense study and elaboration of the divine law. Although the aim of the priests was the preservation of the holy community within an alien environment, they looked forward to the day when Israel should return from exile and be re-established as God's people on the soil that God had given them. Thus their life acquired a certain unreal character, and the law was divorced from its cultural milieu.

Prophetic Insights

Frequently, darkness seems most intense just before the dawn. Jeremiah had prepared Israel for the crisis of the exile. Reaching into the darkness, Jeremiah lifted God's exiles with the hope that his prophetic vision of a new covenant would be fulfilled. Jeremiah promised that from the darkness of exile the sun of a new covenant relationship between Yahweh and Israel would arise. The heart of this prophecy (31:31–34) describes how Yahweh would lead man to a new and effective knowledge of his God.

Jeremiah did not speak of a new torah; rather, he envisioned a new covenant relationship which would enable men to obey the covenant regulations from an inner motivation. Although Jeremiah's teaching on the nature of the new covenant remains distinctly different from that of Paul, the prophet's exposition marked a great advance in the theology of the Old Testament and represented a giant stride in the preparation for a new law.

Ezekiel, Jeremiah's counterpart in Babylon, insisted that God would renew the covenant, cleansing his people and forming a new heart and spirit within them.[1] Ezekiel reiterated Jeremiah's teaching about the important role of the individual in the new covenant. Man's individual response to God's mercy was to be the human matrix of the renewed covenant. The new covenant was to include new laws (Jer 31:33; Ez 36:27); while waiting for God to carry out the

---
[1] See Ez 36:26–28.

promises of the prophets, however, the people were to observe the law as they knew it.

When the re-establishment of the covenant seemed to be delayed, representatives of tradition maintained and strengthened statutes in the hope of restoring the lost covenant. Imperceptibly, they began to regard the law as a substitute for the covenant. Formerly, the law was the expression of the covenant; now the law became the condition of the restoration of the covenant.

Östborn has suggested that one historical reason for the prediction of a new covenant may have been that prophetical circles realized the impossibility of complying with all the regulations of the torah.[2] Ezekiel's hope that a new heart and a new spirit would enable the people to keep Yahweh's statutes (Ez 11:19–20; 36:26–27) seems to warrant this inference. Likewise, Jeremiah (8:8) implied that the very writing of the law thwarted its realization.[3]

Rise of Lay Leaders

Even before the destruction of the temple the explication of the torah had started to become more than solely the prerogative of the priests. Not only did the conditions accompanying the exile produce a more complex system of laws; the interest of the people as a whole in legal matters grew immensely. If they were really destined to become a nation of priests, then everyone, and not only the priest, should be an expert in the law.

The development of the office of scribe marked a significant step in the adjustment of the attitude toward the law. When the study of the law was regarded as an important duty of *all* the people, a deeper penetration into its inner meaning and ultimate implications resulted. Although the priests still

---

[2] Gunnar Östborn, *Tōrā in the Old Testament*, trans. Cedric Hentschel (Lund: Håkan Ohlssons Boktryckeri, 1945), pp. 152–154.

[3] Jer 31:31–34 seems to strengthen this inference. In the days of the new covenant the law written by Yahweh upon the heart will release men from the slavery of the law written by men on scrolls.

retained their office as leaders in the community, the new elite of lay scribes became the ultimate authority on the whole torah.

Progress Toward Legalism

For those who went into exile all was changed. The king was no more; the temple had been destroyed; the environment was no longer closely bound up with Yahwism. Only one thing remained: the law and its regulations which manifested a union between Yahweh and the people. It is not surprising, therefore, that the law absorbed all the ordinances of religion and became the link with God.

Even though the law was eventually looked upon as an absolute, a certain continuity with the true spirit of the law nonetheless remained. Much later when Jewish scholars, engrossed in the pursuit of wisdom, had apparently forgotten the pristine significance of the torah, Ben Sira gave witness to the fact that the true spirit of the law was not extinct in Israel. Underlying Ben Sira's identification of wisdom and the mosaic law (Sir 24:23), the perceptive reader can discern testimony to the true spirit of the law. The comparison of the law with wisdom (Sir 24:23–27) underscored obedience to God and confidence in his alliance.

Halakic Teaching in the Postexilic Period

Israel, a Law Community

The genius of postexilic religion lay in the punctilious observance of the ritual and of each minute prescription of the law. The prophetic demand that God's law be obeyed had issued in a commonwealth where the first order of business was to do just that in every detail. A cardinal tenet of the postexilic community was that the promises of the covenant were dependent upon Israel's exact obedience to every detail of the written law. Thus the law and the covenant were in-

separable, and the law became the very center of national
life.

Concomitantly with the development of the synagogue, the
services of the scribes (*soferim*) were expanded. Originally the
Hebrew word, *soferim*, was applied to those who knew how to
write, but as the art of writing was the domain of the intelligent, the term eventually denoted wise men. The scribes progressed from the copying of the law, through teaching the
letter of the law, and finally to interpreting the law.

In many instances the *soferim* discovered a gulf between
the law as stated in the torah and the exigencies of daily life.
To bridge the gulf, they used midrash. In its earliest form this
midrash consisted in a verse-by-verse commentary on the
written text which was intended to make the teaching more
precise. The care which the scribes took to connect the
halakah[4] with the written form of the law gives an indication
of the manner in which the law was regarded during this
period. Strict emphasis on the letter ultimately helped to
pave the way toward a slavery of the letter against which
Paul found it necessary to inveigh.

Aggressive Jewish nationalism lay dormant as long as the
torah remained the unchallenged ruling factor in the postexilic life of Israel. However, inherent in Hellenism was an
inexorable challenge to the particularity of the torah. This
challenge did not come only in the form of persecution from
pagan overlords; deeper origins were to be found in the internal conflicts within the Jewish community over the way
that Israel should relate to the cultural and economic life
of its hellenistic environment.

Jewish Parties and Sects

According to the Pharisees, the *halakah* was a specific declaration of the divine will applicable to a given case; each *halakah* bound all who accepted the torah as their supreme guide

---

[4] The *halakah* (*halak*, to walk) showed a man the way he should walk
by explaining how he could obey the law in every detail.

and professed to walk in the way it indicated. One of the unfortunate consequences of this system of interpreting the torah lay in the eventual placing of genuine moral obligations on the same level with ritual and external observances. Since the latter were numerous, it was easy to attribute primary importance to them. The eating of improperly butchered meat, for example, was likely to be regarded as serious a sin as slander.

At heart Pharisaism was legalistic; legalism easily leads to formalism, and formalism to externalism and unreality. In the course of time these defects revealed themselves in at least some phases of Pharisaism. In spite of the abberrations that eventually developed as a result of the pharisaic approach to the law, in its methods of interpretation Pharisaism had discovered a means of making the law reasonable and of adapting it to the needs of the time.

New Testament ethic is firmly rooted in prophetism and Pharisaism. Paul called himself a Pharisee, and though he rejected many pharisaic legal interpretations, his years of studying the torah bore fruit in his penetrating insights into the true nature of the law. The dichotomy between pharisaic and Christian ethics rests upon one fundamental antithesis: the Pharisee held that man was capable of doing God's will, whereas the Christian believed that man must first experience an inner transformation; he must receive a new life (2 Cor 5:17). Then, and only then, is man rendered capable of the divinely human performance required of him.

The origins of the sadducean party are obscure; possibly the group came into being as a result of the impact of Hellenism on the older Jewish culture in Palestine. The earliest evidence of the Sadducees as a distinct party among the Palestinian Jews appears in 162 B.C. when Jonathan combined in his person the highest religious and political authority. Under the Hasmonean rulers who followed Jonathan, the Sadducees and the Pharisees vied with one another in seeking to dominate the Sanhedrin for the opportunity such prestige afforded for the propagation of their particular tenets.

The Sadducees were entrenched religious and civil figures; they were a priestly party, an aristocracy who wanted no innovations or changes of any sort. The sadducean reluctance to change was reflected in their attitude toward the law. They held that the torah had acquired absolute authority only from the oath by which the people had pledged themselves to obey it. However, the binding power of the oath, as they conceived it, did not extend beyond the meaning of the words of the law as understood by their ancestors who had taken the oath. This attitude tended to divorce the law from life and to make observance of the letter of the law the all-important consideration. As a result, religious life became centered in such ritual laws as could be observed literally; formalism characterized the temple rites, and everyday life was regarded as completely secular in character.

While the Sadducees upheld the authority of the written law, they regarded it as little more than a relic of the past. If the torah was the center of the Pharisee's faith, to the Sadducee the torah was the circumference within which practices foreign to Judaism could be encompassed. From a position of strict fidelity to the torah they descended to one of pure expediency. Infringements of the law were taken seriously only when these breaches threatened sadducean prerogatives.

The Pharisees and Sadducees represent two extremes with reference to the torah. They must not be regarded as rigidly structured groups, however; lines of adherence were fluid. At the time of Christ the majority of Jews probably occupied a middle position, not in the sense that they stood half-way between the Pharisees and the Sadducees in fidelity to the law, but in that they assented in a general way to the theories of the Pharisees while unable to comply fully with their prescriptions. Caught in this predicament, the ordinary man frequently found in sadducean adjustments a pragmatic solution to his legal dilemma.

In the vicinity of Jerusalem itself, a vigorous form of sectarianism had established itself on the shores of the Dead Sea. Thus the sect of the scrolls developed from the broad nonconformist movement of sectarian Judaism in the first century before Christ. The followers of the Teacher of Justice bound themselves to practice exactly the letter of the law, in that way atoning for the sinfulness around them. Their zeal for the law and their hope of a new covenantal kingdom led them to revive the ancient notion of the holy war by which the land would be purified of the contamination of pagan cultures. Vowing themselves in absolute obedience to their particular interpretation of the torah, the sectaries regarded themselves as the one true Israel, the heirs of the covenant.

The name "Essene" probably designates a number of groups which had similar beliefs and practices. The community which produced the Dead Sea Scrolls existed between the middle of the second century B.C. and A.D. 68 or 69 and was probably a separatist group within the larger Essene movement.[5] The written torah and its study was the basis of their communal life and the inspiration of their movement. Although this sect was a priestly movement, in religious outlook they had more in common with the Pharisees than with the Sadducees. In some respects, their interpretation of the torah was even more rigid than that of the Pharisees. The pharisaic separation was from defilement and not from institutional Judaism as such. In striving for their particular brand of purity, the Essenes divorced themselves even from institutional Judaism.

Relentless and rigid concentration on obedience to the law was one of the most outstanding characteristics of the sect. Theirs was a legalistic and charismatic piety. Aware of itself as under the law and yet as a community of the spirit, the Qumran sectarians seemed to feel no essential tension between life under the law and life under the spirit. Whereas the concept of the spirit in the scrolls fits neatly within a legalistic

---

[5] Lucetta Mowry, *The Dead Sea Scrolls and the Early Church* (Chicago: The University of Chicago Press, 1962), p. 1.

community, Paul sets the spirit in radical opposition to legal entities.[6] However, the parenetic parts of Paul's epistles provide most striking parallels with analogous developments recorded in the scrolls.

Paul's attitude toward the law was purely Christian; the risen Christ who appeared to him at Damascus caused a radical change in Paul's thinking. Nevertheless, it would seem that the Christianity which Paul found in Damascus was that of converted Essenes. This explains the similarity between Paul's message and that of the Essenes.[7] Pauline legal polemic can be understood only against the background of the currents of Judaism in the period in which Christianity came into being. Essenian thought is one very important part of the total environment into which Paul thrust his synthesis.

The Law and the Problem of Continuity

Israel's life story is inseparably linked to the concepts of covenant and law. The conviction that God called Israel, separated her from the nations, and commissioned her as his servant is integral to this understanding. The law must be evaluated within the context of a salvific love which breaks out of old structures in a creative fulfillment thrust.

The pristine notion of law was that it was a blessing, an invitation to go out from oneself. But the human tendency to reach out and grip reality and bring it down to size resulted in the formulation of static rules completely assimilable by human intelligence. The law began to be considered as a natural patrimony to be defended with the same type of polemic with which one defended the civil entity. Although a certain degree of truth characterized this tenet, this concept did not adequately encompass the notion. Concomitant with Israel's belief in her prized legal possession, there always re-

---

6 William D. Davies, Christian Origins and Judaism (Philadelphia: The Westminster Press, 1962), pp. 174–175.

7 Jean Daniélou, The Dead Sea Scrolls and Primitive Christianity, trans. Salvator Attansio (Baltimore: Helicon Press, Inc., 1958), p. 103.

mained an element of fruitful tension between the already and the not yet. Particularly in the resistance movements that were born when Jewish nationalism was threatened there could be discerned a straining, a looking forward to a new covenant, which would bring with it a new law.

Vaguely, but nonetheless surely, the idea of the law became intimately connected with a messianic hope. With all its variety, a real unity persisted through changes of the most far-reaching kind in the notion of a God-given torah. At the very point where the continuity seems decisively broken, where the old covenant gives place to a new testament, deeper study of the concept yields the conviction that the apparent discontinuity masks a very real continuity between the old law and the new law.

BIBLIOGRAPHY

CHAPTER I — St. Paul's Antithetic Presentation of the Law

Ahern, Barnabas M., "The Lord's Freedman," The Way, 2:3 (July, 1962), 166–176.

Barclay, William, Flesh and Spirit: An Examination of Galatians 5:19–23 (Nashville: Abingdon Press, 1962).

Barr, James, The Semantics of Biblical Language (London: Oxford University Press, 1961).

Barrett, C. K., From First Adam to Last: A Study in Pauline Theology (London: Adam and Charles Black, 1962).

Barth, Karl, A Shorter Commentary on Romans (Richmond: John Knox Press, 1959).

Boman, Thorleif, Hebrew Thought Compared with Greek, translated by Jules L. Moreau (London: SCM Press, Ltd., 1960).

Bultmann, Rudolf, Theology of the New Testament, I, translated by Kendrick Grobel (New York: Charles Scribner's Sons, 1951).

Cranfield, C. E. B., "St. Paul and the Law," Scottish Journal of Theology, 17:1 (March, 1964), 43–68.

Dodd, C. H., Gospel and Law (New York: Columbia University Press, 1951).

Gale, Herbert M., The Use of Analogy in the Letters of Paul (Philadelphia: The Westminster Press, 1964).

George, Augustin, La Morale de Paul: Études Exegétiques (Paris: Commission des Études Religieuses, 1959).

Graham, Holt, "Continuity and Discontinuity in the Thought of St. Paul," Anglican Theological Review, 38:2 (April, 1956, 137–146.

Grant, Frederick C., Roman Hellenism and the New Testament (New York: Charles Scribner's Sons, 1962).

Johnson, Sherman E., "Paul and the Manual of Discipline," Harvard Theological Review, 48:3 (July, 1955), 157–165.

Knox, John, The Ethic of Jesus in the Teaching of the Church (Nashville: Abingdon Press, 1961).

Leenhardt, Franz J., The Epistle to the Romans, translated by Harold Knight (London: Lutterworth Press, 1961).

Longenecker, Richard N., Paul: Apostle of Liberty (New York: Harper and Row, Publishers, 1964).

Mead, Charles M., Irenic Theology: A Study of Some Antitheses in Religious Thought (New York: G. P. Putnam's Sons, 1905).

Ramsey, Ian T., Religious Language: An Empirical Placing of Theological Phrases (London: SCM Press, Ltd., 1957).

Robinson, John A. T., The Body: A Study in Pauline Theology (London: SCM Press, 1952).

Schneider, Bernardin, "The Meaning of St. Paul's Antithesis 'The Letter and the Spirit,'" The Catholic Biblical Quarterly, 15:2 (April, 1953), 163–207.

Schoeps, Hans Joachim, *Paul: The Theology of the Apostle in the Light of Jewish Religious History*, translated by Harold Knight (London: Lutterworth Press, 1961).

Sevenster, J. N., "Paul and Seneca," *Supplements to Novum Testamentum*, Vol. IV (Leiden: E. J. Brill, 1961).

Tresmontant, Claude, *A Study of Hebrew Thought*, translated by Michael Francis Gibson (New York: Desclée Company, 1960).

Whiteley, Denys Edward, *The Theology of St. Paul* (Philadelphia: Fortress Press, 1964).

CHAPTER II — Tripartite Christian Law

Andersen, Wilhelm, *Law and Gospel: A Study in Biblical Theology* (New York: Association Press, 1961).

Barr, James, *The Semantics of Biblical Language* (London: Oxford University Press, 1961).

Brunner, Emil, *The Letter to the Romans* (Philadelphia: The Westminster Press, 1959).

Bushell, Gerard, "Law and Christian Spirituality According to St. Paul," *Australian Biblical Review*, 5:3–4 (December, 1956), 99–117.

Daniélou, Jean, *The Theology of Jewish Christianity*, translated and edited by John A. Baker (Chicago: The Henry Regnery Company, 1964).

Grossouw, W., "L'Espérance dans le Nouveau Testament," *Revue Biblique*, 61:4 (October, 1954), 508–532.

Knox, John, *Life in Christ Jesus* (Greenwich: The Seabury Press, 1961).

Lampe, G. W. H., "The Atonement: Law and Love," *Soundings: Essays Concerning Christian Understanding*, edited by A. R. Vidler (Cambridge: University Press, 1962), pp. 175–191.

Lyonnet, Stanislas, "St. Paul: Liberty and Law," *The Bridge*, IV, edited by John M. Oesterreicher (New York: Pantheon Books, 1962), 229–251.

Quell, Gottfried, and Stauffer, Ethelbert, "ἀγαπάω, ἀγάπη, ἀγαπητός," *Theological Dictionary of the New Testament*, I, edited by Gerhard Kittel and translated by Geoffrey Bromiley (Grand Rapids: Wm. B. Eerdmans Publishing Company, 1964), pp. 21–55.

Schnackenburg, Rudolf, *The Moral Teaching of the New Testament*, translated by J. Holland-Smith and W. J. O'Hara (New York: Herder and Herder, 1965).

Sloyan, Gerard S., "Faith and Modern Subjective Thought," *Proceedings of the Eighteenth Annual Convention of the Catholic Theological Society of America* (New York: The Catholic Theological Society of America, 1964), pp. 77–87.

Spicq, Ceslaus, "La Morale Neótestamentaire: Morale Chrétienne et Morale de la Charité," *Neotestamentica et Patristica. Supplements* to *Novum Testamentum*, VI (Leiden: E. J. Brill, 1962), pp. 228–239.

CHAPTER III — Essential Freedom of Life in the Spirit

Cambier, Jules, "La Liberté Chrétienne selon Saint Paul," *Lumière et Vie*, 12:61 (Janvier-Février, 1963), 5–40.

Cerfaux, L., *Le Chrétien dans la Théologie Paulinienne* (Paris: Les Éditions du Cerf, 1962).

Festugière, André, *Liberté et Civilisation chez les Grecs* (Paris: Éditions de la Revue des Jeunes, 1947).

Goguel, Maurice, *The Primitive Church*, translated by H. C. Snape (New York: The Macmillan Company, 1964).

Güemes, Agapito, "La ΕΛΕΥΘΕΡΙΑ en las Epistolas Paulinas," *Estudios Biblicos*, 21:1 (Enero-Marzo, 1962), 37–63.

Lüthi, Walter, *The Letter to the Romans* (Richmond: John Knox Press, 1961).

Mouroux, Jean, *The Christian Experience*, translated by George Lamb (New York: Sheed and Ward, 1954).

Munck, Johannes, *Paul and the Salvation of Mankind*, translated by Frank Clarke (London: SCM Press, Ltd., 1959).

Oden, Thomas, *Radical Obedience* (Philadelphia: The Westminster Press, 1964).

Rengstorf, Karl H., "δοῦλος," *Theological Dictionary of the New Testament*, II, edited by Gerhard Kittel and translated by Geoffrey W. Bromiley (Grand Rapids: Wm. B. Eerdmans Publishing Company, 1964), pp. 261–280.

Schlier, Heinrich, "ἐλεύθερος," *Theological Dictionary of the New Testament*, II, edited by Gerhard Kittel and translated by Geoffrey W. Bromiley (Grand Rapids: Wm. B. Eerdmans Publishing Company, 1964), pp. 487–502.

Spicq, Ceslaus, *Charity and Liberty in the New Testament*, translated by Francis V. Manning (Staten Island: St. Paul Publications, 1965).

——— "La Liberté selon le Nouveau Testament," *Sciences Ecclésiastiques*, 12:2 (1960), 229–240.

Stanley, David Michael, *Christ's Resurrection in Pauline Soteriology* (Romae, e Pontificio Instituto Biblico, 1961).

Tcherikover, Victor, *Hellenistic Civilization and the Jews*, translated by S. Applebaum (Philadelphia: The Jewish Publication Society of America, 1959).

Wood, Arthur Skevington, *Life by the Spirit* (Grand Rapids: Zondervan Publishing House, 1963).

CHAPTER IV — Contemporary Moral Catechesis

Altizer, Thomas J. J., *Mircea Eliade and the Dialectic of the Sacred* (Philadelphia: The Westminster Press, 1963).

Bergson, Henrí, *The Two Sources of Morality and Religion*, translated by R. Ashley Audra and Cloudesley Brereton (London: Macmillan and Co., Ltd., 1935).

Bonhoeffer, Dietrich, *Prisoner for God*, edited by Eberhard Bethge and translated by Reginald Fuller (New York: The Macmillan Company, 1954).

Brunner, Emil, *Man in Revolt*, translated by Olive Wyon (Philadelphia: The Westminster Press, 1957).

Cirne-Lima, Carlos, *Personal Faith*, translated by G. Richard Dimler (New York: Herder and Herder, 1965).

Coiner, Harry, "Law and Gospel in Christian Education," *Concordia Theological Monthly*, 35:10 (November, 1964), 622–631.

Cox, Harvey, *The Secular City* (New York: The Macmillan Company, 1965).

Curran, Charles E., *Christian Morality Today* (Notre Dame: Fides Publishers, Inc., 1966).

Dondeyne, Albert, *Faith and the World*, translated by Walter van de Putte (Pittsburgh: Duquesne University Press, 1963).

Gustafson, James, "Context versus Principles: A Misplaced Debate in Christian Ethics," *Harvard Theological Review*, 58:2 (April, 1965), 171–202.

Häring, Bernard, *Toward a Christian Moral Theology* (Notre Dame: University of Notre Dame Press, 1966).

Lepp, Ignace, *The Authentic Morality*, translated by Bernard Murchland (New York: The Macmillan Company, 1965).

Monden, Louis, *Sin, Liberty and Law*, translated by Joseph Donceel (New York: Sheed and Ward, 1965).

Moule, C. F. D., "The New Testament and Moral Decisions," *The Expository Times*, 74:12 (September, 1963), 370–373.

Nebreda, Alfonso, "Living Faith: Major Concern of Religious Education," *Pastoral Catechetics*, edited by Johannes Hofinger and Theodore Stone (New York: Herder and Herder, 1964), pp. 121–143.

Oraison, Marc, *Love or Constraint?* translated by Una Morrissy (New York: P. J. Kenedy and Sons, 1959).

Rahner, Karl, "On the Question of a Formal Existential Ethics," *Theological Investigations*, Vol. II: *Man in the Church*, translated by Karl-H. Kruger (Baltimore: Helicon Press, 1963), 217–234.

Schreibmayr, Franz, "The Faith of the Church and Formal Doctrinal Instruction," *Modern Catechetics*, edited by Gerard Sloyan (New York: The Macmillan Company, 1963), pp. 45–62.

Teilhard de Chardin, Pierre, *L'Énergie Humaine* (Paris: Éditions du Seuil, 1962).

——— *The Future of Man*, translated by Norman Denny (New York: Harper and Row, Publishers, 1964).

Tillich, Paul, *Dynamics of Faith* (New York: Harper and Brothers Publishers, 1957).

Walgrave, Jan, "Is Morality Static or Dynamic?" translated by Theodore L. Westow, *Moral Problems and Christian Personalism*, Vol. V of *Concilium* (New York: Paulist Press, 1965), 22–38.

CHAPTER V — Liberty, Hallmark of Christian Contemporary Life

Adler, Alfred, *Social Interest: A Challenge to Mankind*, translated by John Linton and Richard Vaughan (London: Faber and Faber, Ltd., 1938).

Allen, G. Margery, "The Adlerian Interpretation of Compulsion," *Essays in Individual Psychology*, edited by Kurt Adler and Danica Deutsch (New York: Grove Press, Inc., 1959), pp. 55–58.

Ansbacher, Heinz and Rowena (eds.), *The Individual Psychology of Alfred Adler* (New York: Basic Books, Inc., 1956).

Chamberlin, J. Gordon, *Freedom and Faith: New Approaches to Christian Education* (Philadelphia: The Westminster Press, 1965).

Curran, Charles, "Theological Foundations for a Spiritual Formation in Freedom and Responsibility," *Proceedings: Society of Catholic College Teachers of Sacred Doctrine* (Weston: Society of Catholic College Teachers of Sacred Doctrine, 1965), pp. 164–176.

Dietrich, Suzanne de, "Captives into Children: The Biblical Doctrine of Freedom," *Interpretation*, 6:4 (October, 1952), 387–389.

Freud, Sigmund, *An Autobiographical Study*, translated by James Strachey (London: Hogarth Press, 1946).

——— *The Ego and the Id*, translated by Joan Riviere (London: Hogarth Press, 1949).

——— *The Problem of Anxiety*, translated by Henry Alden Bunker (New York: The Psychoanalytic Quarterly Press, 1936).

Gogarten, Friedrich, *The Reality of Faith*, translated by Carl Michalson and others (Philadelphia: The Westminster Press, 1959).

Gustafson, James, "Christian Ethics," *Religion*, edited by Paul Ramsey (Englewood Cliffs: Prentice-Hall, Inc., 1965), pp. 287–354.

Jocz, Jakób, *A Theology of Election: Israel and the Church* (London: S.P.C.K., 1958).

Mailloux, Noël, "Psychic Determinism, Freedom, and Personality Development," *Canadian Journal of Psychology*, 7:1 (March, 1953), 1–11.

Niebuhr, H. Richard, *The Responsible Self* (New York: Harper and Row, Publishers, 1963).

Thompson, J. A., "The Near Eastern Suzerain-Vassal Concept in the Religion of Israel," *The Journal of Religious History*, 3:1 (June, 1964), 1–16.

Walgrave, John, *Person and Society: A Christian View*, translated by Walter van de Putte (Pittsburgh: Duquesne University Press, 1965).

APPENDIX — Some Background for Paul's Teaching
on the Law

Brownlee, William Hugh, *The Meaning of the Qumran Scrolls for the Bible* (New York: Oxford University Press, 1964).

Cullmann, Oscar, "The Significance of the Qumran Texts for Research into the Beginnings of Christianity," *Journal of Biblical Literature*, 74:4 (December, 1955), 213–226.

Daniélou, Jean, *The Dead Sea Scrolls and Primitive Christianity* (Baltimore: Helicon Press, Inc., 1958).

Davies, William D., *Christian Origins and Judaism* (Philadelphia: The Westminster Press, 1962).

———— *Torah in the Messianic Age and/or the Age to Come* ("Journal of Biblical Literature Monograph Series," Vol. VII) (Philadelphia: Society of Biblical Literature, 1952).

Dumont, Enrique, "La Ley mosaica y su abolicion," *Revista Biblica*, 22:95 (Enero–Marzo, 1960), 1–7; 22:96 (Abril–Junio, 1960), 82–88.

Jaubert, Annie, *La Notion d'Alliance dans le Judaïsme* (Paris: Éditions du Seuil, 1963).

Mowry, Lucetta, *The Dead Sea Scrolls and the Early Church* (Chicago: The University of Chicago Press, 1962).

North, Robert, "The Qumran 'Sadducees,'" *The Catholic Biblical Quarterly*, 17:2 (April, 1955), 164–168.

O'Connell, Matthew, "The Concept of Commandment in the Old Testament," *Theological Studies*, 21:3 (September, 1960), 351–403.

Östborn, Gunnar, *Tōrā in the Old Testament* (Lund: Håkan Ohlssons Boktryckeri, 1945).

Rabin, Chaim, *Qumran Studies* (London: Oxford University Press, 1957).

Rowley, Harold H., "The Qumran Sect and Christian Origins," *Bulletin of the John Rylands Library*, 44:1 (September, 1961), 119–156.

INDEX

Action, baptismal, 74; paschal, 72
Adler, Alfred, 110; determinism and indeterminism, 113 ff
Agápē, see Love
Alienation, 78, 109
Anomía, see Sin
Anthropocentism, 103
Antinomism, 92
Antithesis, 20, 26; of flesh and spirit, 14, 16; of letter and spirit, 17, 22; of life and death, 17; Paul's love of, 3 ff
Atonement, 123

Baptism, 76 f, 92 ff, 96, 100, 129 f; and hope, 46; liberating power of, 52; sharing in Christ's death and resurrection, 42, 74
Bonhoeffer, Dietrich, sacred and profane, 81

Catechesis, and dynamic character of Christian morality, 91 f; moral, 78 ff, 122; of prayer, 101 ff; on sin, 88 f; systematic, 95 f
Catechist, and morality, 80; moral teaching of, 103 ff; and Paul's example, 99; role in teaching morality, 85
Christ, 98 f, 128 f; cosmic view of, 85; death of, 15, 16; law of, 48 ff; leads men to view relations with God, 82 f; the new law, 131; sacrament, 105; spirit of, 20
Christian, led by spirit of love, 98; moral catechesis of, 102; norm for, 105; what it means to be a, 84
Christianity, 87, 141; a message of love, 96 f
Church, 123; new creation, 46
Circumcision, 20 f, 61, 107
Commandments, and love, 99
Communion, state of, 100
Community, 47, 86, 107, 121 ff, 127 ff, 134, 136; in Christ, 46, 102; Christian, 49, 67 ff, 72, 77, 118; Freudian concept, 112; and individual, 91; and love, 43
Consecration, baptismal, 96
Contextualism, see Existentialism

Covenant, 29, 33, 74, 102, 116, 126 ff, 134 f, 141 f; baptismal, 99; Christ and, 49 f; and community, 15; and law, 136 f; new, 32 f; new, of freedom, 28; old and new, 17 f, 20

Dead Sea Scrolls, 13 f, 140
Death, 17, 84; conquered by Christ, 72 ff; freedom from, 76; of the Lord, 101; and sin, 14 f, 116 f
Despair, 106
Determinism, 110 ff
Doûlos, see Slavery

Education, Christian, 121; Christian moral, 91 f, 102; moral, 133; of St. Paul, 55
Election, 101, 126 ff; end of the law, 130 f
Emotions, 114
Encounter, 95, 102
Éros, see Love
Éschaton, 99
Essenes, see Qumran sectaries
Eternity, 128
Ethics, 98; Christian, 24, 49, 80; Christian moral, 85; New Testament, 138; pagan, 24; and religion, 30
Eucharist, 101 f, 104 f, 123, 129
Existentialism, 80, 90
Exodus, baptism and new, 99
Expectation, Christian, 100 ff

Faith, 17, 40, 44, 76 f, 93 ff, 133; Christian, 28, 90; foundation of Christian existence, 36 ff; and freedom, 53; looks to love, 106
Flesh, 19 f; obedience to, 67; Paul's meaning of, 63; Paul's notion of, 10 f; and spirit, 8 ff, 14; various concepts of, 12 ff; versus spirit, 11 f, 16
Freedom, 19, 25, 43; background to Paul's teaching on, 51 ff; in Christ, 15; Christian, 7, 21 ff, 24, 26, 67 ff, 109, 117 ff, 124 ff; divine, 97; and grace, 59; human, 106 f, 110 ff; and law, 10 ff, 107 f; libera-